Bengali

lonely planet

phrasebooks

Bimal Maity

Bengali phrasebook
1st edition – January 1996

Published by
Lonely Planet Publications Pty Ltd ABN 36 005 607 983
90 Maribyrnong St, Footscray, Victoria 3011, Australia

Lonely Planet Offices
Australia Locked Bag 1, Footscray, Victoria 3011
USA 150 Linden St, Oakland CA 94607
UK 72-82 Rosebery Ave, London, EC 1R 4RW
France 1 rue du Dahomey, 75011 Paris

This book was written by Bimal Maity and edited by Louise Callan. Penelope Richardson was responsible for design and inside illustrations. The cover illustration is by Cameron Hehir and the cover design by Yukiyoshi Kamimura. Thanks to Rathin Mukherjee for proofreading. The author gratefully acknowledges the help of Chobi Hossain and the support of his wife Renu and daughter Mohona.

ISBN 0 86442 312 8

10 9 8 7 6 5 4 3 2

Printed through Colorcraft Ltd, Hong Kong
Printed in China

Contents

Introduction

Bengali is the national language of Bangladesh and the official language of the state of West Bengal in India. There are also Bengali-speaking communities in many of the north-eastern states of India. It is spoken by a staggering total of 220 million people.

Like other languages of the subcontinent, Bengali is an Indo-Aryan language which is the easternmost language group within Indo-European. Modern Bengali is derived from Sanskrit, a sister language to Greek and one of the earliest recorded languages of the Indo-European group. It was the principal language of religious writings and scholarship on the Indian subcontinent and is now recognised as one of the languages for official use in the modern state of India. Although the Bengali language dates back centuries, it was not well known to the rest of the world until Rabindra Nath Thakur (known as Tagore to the Western world) won the Nobel Prize for literature in 1913. Pride in the Bengali language became one of the chief factors in the struggle for independence in India and Bangaldesh. As such, Bengali is a language which is very rich in cultural and literary content. In fact, it was the first of the Indian

Rabindranath Tagore

languages to develop Western literary styles of fiction and drama; even sonnets and odes were written in Bengali.

Like all languages, Bengali has numerous regional dialects. There are two very distinctive dialects, however. Sadhu-bhasa is the literary language which uses many Sanskrit words and is unintelligible to those who have not been educated in it. Calit-bhasa is the colloquial speech and is based on the dialect of Calcutta. It is spoken and understood by all Bengali speakers. In this book, we have used Calit-bhasa which is universally understood throughout Bengali-speaking communities. It is also the language of the media and of education.

You will find that Bengalis who know some English will be very keen to practise it with you. If you find yourself in a situation where you are unable to express a phrase, just point to the relevant script on the right hand side of the page. Unless otherwise indicated, the polite form of address has been used throughout this phrasebook.

Abbreviations Used In This Book

(a) – adjective
(B) – this word is particular to Bangladesh
(f) – feminine
(inf) – informal
(int) – intimate form of address
(lit) – literally
(m) – masculine
(n) – noun
(pl) – plural

(p) – polite form of address
(S) – Sadhu-bhasa dialect
(s) – subject
(sg) – singular
(v) – verb

Help!

To help you get started, here are a few basic words in Bengali you should try to memorise. The word *nomoskār* is both the Hindu greeting and goodbye. You say this as you bring your palms together in front of your chest. The Muslim greeting is *ādāb* which you say while touching your forehead with the palm of your right hand. 'Thank you' is *dhonyobād* and 'Please' is *doyākōre* although you won't hear these words used in the same way as in English. See Greetings & Civilities for more details on this.

Use *māf kōrben* for 'Excuse me'. 'Yes' is *h̃ā* and 'No' is *nā*. If you run into language difficulties see page 36 and try to remember the phrase *bujhte pārlām nā* which means 'I don't understand'.

Good luck!
subhayo bhobotu!

Pronunciation

Bengali, like many of the languages of South Asia, is rich with sounds. Many of these are not present in English and are, therefore, difficult to grasp. The positioning of the tongue and lips when pronouncing some sounds in Bengali is unusual for English speakers.

This chapter provides a description of the sounds you will encounter in the Bengali language and an explanation of the physical apparatus used to make each sound, ie how to position your tongue and lips. With a little practice you will soon be competent enough with Bengali pronunciation to be able to communicate with the locals.

Transliteration

The transliterations (Romanisation) of Bengali script used in this book have particular marks above and/or below some letters which are not found in the Roman alphabet. These are called diacritics and they indicate a variation of a sound. For instance, a line above a letter (known as a macron, eg *ā)* denotes a long vowel sound. (Note the difference between the short 'a' in 'cat' and the long 'a' sound in 'father'. A squiggly line above a letter (known as a tilde, eg *ã)* denotes a nasal sound like the 'ny' in the Spanish *señor*. A dot under a 't' *(ṭ)* or a 'd' *(ḍ)* indicates that it is a retroflex sound and a dot under an 'r' *(ṛ)* indicates a retroflex flap. Retroflex sounds are explained on page 9.

Methods of Pronunciation

Here are some explanations of how sounds unfamiliar to the English speaker are formed.

Gutterals

The tongue blocks part of the pharynx so that the sound comes from the back of the throat – like gagging at the dentist.

Palatals

The sides and front of the tongue are pressed against the roof of the mouth as in the pronunciation of the English 'j'.

Retroflex

The tongue is curled back behind the alveolar ridge on the roof of the mouth. A retroflex flap is a quick flap of the tongue in retroflex position.

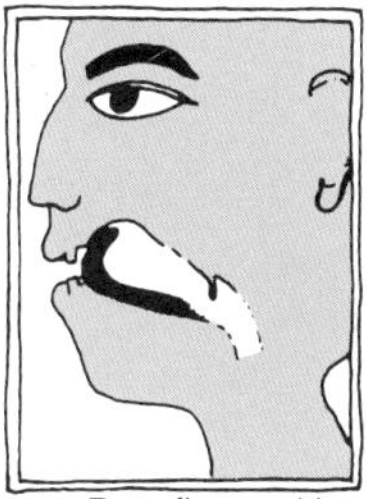

Retroflex position

Dentals

The tongue is pressed behind the upper teeth as for the English 'd' and 't'.

Labials

A method of making a sound that involves movement or use of the lips, eg 'f'.

Vowels

There are 11 vowels in the Bengali alphabet. Apart from the five basic vowels as in the Roman alphabet, there are two long vowels and two common vowel combinations (diphthongs). Unlike most diphthongs in English which combine to form a new sound, each vowel in a diphthong in Bengali keeps its own sound. There are two distinct sounds, therefore, when two or more vowels are combined in Bengali.

Bengali also uses an 'inherent' vowel. When consonants are pronounced on their own, or when they appear as the last letter of a word, they are followed by the vowel sound 'o' (as in the British 'h**o**t'). This is called an inherent vowel. In English we use inherent vowel sounds to pronounce most consonants. For example, the letter 'b' is pronounced b**ee**, 'd' (d**ee**), 'l' (**e**l), 'j' (j**ay**).

a as in 'c**a**t'
ā as in 'f**ar**'
e as in 'b**e**d'
i as in '**i**nn'
o as in 'sh**o**t'. This is also the inherent vowel.
ō as in 'r**o**le'
u as in 'b**oo**k'

Diphthongs

ōi two sounds together (as in 't**oyi**ng')
ōu two sounds together

Consonants

Consonants in Bengali are grouped into five different categories, depending on the way they are pronounced. The differences in these pronunciation methods are subtle.

Furthermore, almost all consonants in Bengali have two forms – aspirated and unaspirated. An 'h' after a consonant in the transliterations indicates that the consonant is aspirated. When a sound is aspirated, it is pronounced with a puff of unvoiced air, eg the 'p' in 'party' and the 't' in 'top'. If you put your hand to your mouth when you say these words you can feel the air escaping. The 't' and 'p' in 'stop', however, are unaspirated. In Bengali, aspirated consonants must be well stressed, that is, a forceful rush of air (like a strongly sounded 'h') must follow the sound.

Consonants are pronounced as in English except for the following:

s	as in '**sh**ine'
ṭ and *ḍ*	are retroflex sounds
ṭh and *ḍh*	are aspirated retroflex sounds
ṛ	is used to denote the retroflex flap which sounds a little like the 'd' in 'ladder'. There is no real equivalent sound in English.
c	as in '**ch**in'
ng	as in 'si**ng**er'
j	as in the English 'j' or as in '**y**oga'. There is no simple rule as to which way this is pronounced.

Stress

This is very subtle in Bengali and there are regional variations as to which part of a word is stressed. When starting off, it is not necessary to know the intricacies of stress and intonation in Bengali. You will be understood without worrying too much about it.

Grammar

This chapter introduces the basics of Bengali grammar, to help you understand the phrases you are using and enable you to put together your own sentences.

Sentence Structure

There is a consistent word order in Bengali – subject-object-verb. All sentences begin with the subject and end with the verb. This rule does not change, even for questions and negative sentences.

I know Bengali.	*āmi bānglā jāni* (lit: I Bengali know)
I don't know Bengali.	*āmi bānglā jāni nā* (lit: I Bengali know not)
Do you know Bengali?	*tumi bānglā jāno?* (lit: you Bengali know?)

Articles

The definite article ('the') in Bengali is used only for added emphasis, otherwise it is omitted altogether. When used, it takes the form of a suffix, *-ṭa* or *-ṭi*, which is added to the noun.

book	*bōi*
the book	*bōiṭi/bōiṭā*
boy	*chele*
the boy	*cheleṭi*

The indefinite article is formed by joining *ak* ('one') with the definite article. This is the equivalent of 'a/an' in English but is only used in Bengali when you want to particularly emphasise that there is one of something:

I want an apple. (just one)	*āmi **akṭā** āpel cāi*
They have a son. (only one)	*ōdher **akṭi** chele āche*

Nouns

Bengali nouns do not have genders as in French or German. However, there is a pattern to gender-specific nouns. *ā*, *i* or *ii* is added to the masculine form of the word to create the feminine form:

deer	*horin*
doe	*horin**ii***

Plurals

Plurals are formed by adding *-rā* to nouns and pronouns representing people, *der* to possessive pronouns and *guli*, *gulō* or *gulā* to inanimate objects.

boy/boys	*chele/chele**rā***
book/books	*bōi/bōi**guli***

Adjectives & Adverbs

Both adjectives and adverbs precede the noun or verb they describe.

red mango	***lāl** ām*
walk **fast**	***jōre** colun*

GRAMMAR

Pronouns

Personal pronouns in the second person ('you') singular and plural have three forms – polite, informal and intimate. The third person singular and plural pronouns ('he/she/they') have two – polite and informal.

Personal Pronouns

	Polite	Informal	Intimate
I	*āmi*		
you (sg)	*āpni*	*tumi*	*tui*
he/she	*tini*	*se*	
we	*āmrā*		
you (pl)	*āpnārā*	*tomrā*	*torā*
they	*t̃ārā*	*tārā*	

Possessive Pronouns

	Polite	Informal	Intimate
my	*āmār*		
your	*āpnār*	*tōmār*	*tōr*
his/her	*t̃ar*	*tār*	*tār*
our	*āmāder*		
your	*āpnāder*	*tōmāder*	*tōder*
their	*t̃āder*	*tāder*	*tāder*

To express possession in Bengali, use the possessive pronoun, not the subject pronoun as you would in English.

She has a cat. ***tār*** *ikṭā beṛāl āche*

Demonstrative Pronouns

The forms vary depending on whether the person or thing referred to is near or far.

Near	Polite	Informal
this person	*ini*	*e*
these persons	*enārā*	*erā*
Far		
that person	*uni*	*ō*
those persons	*ōnārā*	*ōrā*

Verbs

Present

This tense is used for habitual present actions, eg 'I don't drink' or 'She plays the piano everyday'. The general rule to form the present tense is to drop the final vowel from the infinitive form (dictionary form) of the verb. This gives you the verb stem. Then add the following endings:

I & we	*-i*
you (sg & pl)	*-o*
he/she & they	*-e* (inf)/*-en* (p)

to eat — *khāoyā*
I eat rice. — *āmi bhāt* ***khāi***

to play — *khelā*
He plays ball. — *se* (inf) *bol* ***khele***

Present & Past Continuous

This tense is used for actions and events taking place at the present time or one that went on for an amount of time in the past, eg 'The sun is shining' and 'I was writing a letter (when he entered the room)'.

Once you know the form of the verb for the first person, you can work out the forms for the other subjects. The formation of the present and past continous is complex but if you remember that there is always a *ch* sound near the end of the verb, you will be able to recognise these tenses. The endings for the present continuous are formed by adding *-ch* or *-cch* plus the present tense endings to the verb stem. To make the past continuous add *-ch* or *-cch* plus the following endings:

I & we	*-ilām*
you (sg & pl)	*-ile*
he/she & they	*-ilo*

I am doing.	*āmi korchi*
I was doing.	*āmi korchilām*
She is eating.	*tini khācchen*
The dog was sleeping.	*kukurṭi ghumācche*

Future

The endings for this are:

I & we	*bō*
you (sg & pl)	*be*
he/she & they	*ben/be* (inf)

You will come.	*tumi* (inf) *āsbe*
I will mend it tomorrow.	*āmi kāl ōṭā sārābō*

Past Participle

The past participle is a form of the verb that expresses a past state. In English it is used with the verb 'to have' or 'to be' to form a compound past tense, eg in the sentence 'I have eaten', 'eaten' is the past participle. In 'I have seen', 'seen' is the past participle. It can also be used adjectivally or to express the passive, eg 'Rice is eaten at every meal'.

The past participle in Bengali is simple. The sound *e* is added to the infinitive of the verb:

Infinitive	Past Participle
lekha (to write)	*likhe* (written)
khāoyā (to eat)	*kheye* (eaten)
dhōyā (to wash)	*dhuy*e (washed)

In Bengali, past participles are also used:

- to connect two verbs where you would use a conjunction in English:

I went to bed after I washed the dishes.	*āmi bāson* ***dhuye*** *sute gelām*

- to join two clauses that in English would be introduced by words such as 'when' or 'after':

Go to bed after finishing your meal.	*khāōār* ***pōṛe*** *ghumōte jāo*

Past

The past participle is also used to form the past tense in Bengali.

I came to ... seven years ago.	*āmi sāt bochor āge ...* ***esechilām*** (lit: I seven years ago to ... came)
They worked very hard today.	*ōrā āj khub* ***kheṭeche*** (lit: they today very hard worked)

GRAMMAR

Imperatives

As for all other verb forms there are both formal and informal imperatives (commands). Bengali distinguishes between present and future imperatives. In English we only have the present imperative. The general rule for forming the imperative is to add *-o* (inf) or *-un* (p) to the verb stem for the present and *-be* (inf) or *-ben* (p) for the future. Here is an example using the verb *lekha* ('to write'):

Present	Future
lekho (inf)	*likhbe* (inf)
likhun (p)	*likhben* (p)

A Few Pointers

Understanding how to form verb tenses in Bengali is rather complex. To make things a bit simpler, there are just a few general tips to remember so that you are able to recognise the different tenses when you hear them:

- All formal forms of address use an 'n' at the end.

You do.	*āpni kore**n***

- The past tense will have an *l* sound and the future tense will have a *b* sound.

He did.	*se* (inf) *kōr**lō***
He will do.	*se* (inf) *kōr**be***

- An extra *e* is added before the *ch* sound in the past tense.

I have done.	*āmi kore**chi***
I did.	*āmi kore**chilām***

To Be & To Have

The verb 'to be' is not used in Bengali as it is in English. A sentence such as 'Peter is happy' does not require a verb in Bengali. It is simply expressed then as 'Peter happy'.

Bimal is very naughty. — *Bimal khub dushṭu* (lit: Bimal very naughty)

The verb *āch* is used to denote presence. In this way it is like 'to be':

She is here. — *se* (inf) *ekhāne* ***āche*** (lit: she here is)

It is also used to express possession and in this way it acts like 'to have' in English:

I have a car. — *āmār akṭā gā i* ***āche*** (lit: I a car have)

Questions

To turn a statement into a question you can just use the tone of your voice or you can use the words *-ki* or *-nāki* at the end of the sentence. Which to use is just a matter of personal preference:

Where do you work? — *āpni kōthāy kāj koren?* (just using intonation)

Do you have a dog? — *tōmār* (inf) *kukur āche* ***ki****?*

Question Words

These are often used as prefixes in Bengali.

how	*koto-*
which/what	*je-*
when	*kokhon*
where	*kōthāy*
why	*kano*
who	*ke* (sg)/ *kārā* (pl)

How many bananas? ***koto**gulō kolā?*
Where is the money? *tākā **kōthāy**?*

Particles

These words, used as prefixes or suffixes in Bengali, are used quantitatively:

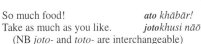

that much	*oto-*
how much	*koto-*
so much	*ato-*
as much	*joto-*
as much as	*toto-*

So much food! ***ato** khābār!*
Take as much as you like. ***joto**khusi nāō*
(NB *joto-* and *toto-* are interchangeable)

Negatives

Use *nā* at the end of the sentence to make it negative:

He will not come. *tini āsben **nā***

Prepositions

These are actually postpositions in Bengali as they are joined to the end of the noun.

in	*-o/-e*
on/to	*-e*
at	*-te*
for	*-jonno*
from	*-theke/-hōte*

Conjunctions

and	*ebong/ō*
but	*kintu*
because	*jehetu*

Some Useful Words

about	*sombondhe*
after	*pore*
before	*āge*
if	*jodi*
towards	*dike*
up to	*porjonto*
with	*songe*

Greetings & Civilities

Greetings vary in Bengali according to religion and custom. Hindus say *nomoskār* when greeting and saying goodbye. This is accompanied by the gesture of joining the open palms of both hands and bringing them close to the chest. When Muslims greet each other they lift the open palm of the right hand to touch their forehead and say *ādāb*, *sālām-ā-lekum* or *ālekum sālām*. A greeting is not always a simple 'hello' or 'goodbye'. It may often be an expression of joy, a compliment or a well wishing. The Muslim greeting *sālām-ā-lekum* literally means 'Peace be on you'.

Greetings & Goodbyes

You should generally stick to the more polite forms when greeting people.

Hello.
nomoskār/ādāb — নমস্কার / আদাব
Good morning.
suprovāt — সুপ্রভাত
How are you?
kamon āchen? — কেমন আছেন?
kamon āchō? (inf) — কেমন আছ?
kamon āchish? (int) — কেমন আছিস?
Goodbye.
nomoskār/bidāyo — নমস্কার / বিদায়

I hope we meet again.
ābār dakhā hobe আবার দেখা হবে
Please come again.
ābār āsben আবার আসবেন

Civilities
Bengalis believe that gratitude and politeness should be expressed through actions and tone of voice rather than through verbal expressions. Consequently, terms like 'thank you' or 'please' are not commonly used. The absence of these should not be misread as rudeness. If you want to thank someone, you may use the equivalent Bengali phrase or, alternatively, pay them a compliment.

Thank you (very much).
(onek) dhonyobād অনেক ধন্যবাদ

Please.
doyā kōre দয়া করে
Excuse me.
māf kōrben মাফ করবেন
Well done!
besh kōrechen! বেশ করেছেন
Thank you for taking the trouble.
āpnāke onek kosṭo dilām আপনাকে অনেক কষ্ট দিলাম
(lit: I've given you a lot of trouble)

Reception & Entertaining

You should take off your shoes before entering the inner part of somebody's house. It is considered impolite to refuse an offer of food or drink.

We have come unannounced.
khobor nādiye cōle elām খবর না দিয়ে চলে এলাম
We hope we have not inconvenienced you.
osubidhā kōrlām nā to? অসুবিধা করলাম না ত?
I'd like a drink of water, please.
ak glās jol/pāni (B) *din* এক গ্লাস জল / পানি দিন
I must go now.
āsi/cōli tāhōle আসি / চলি তাহলে
(The word *āsi* literally means 'I will return'. This is often used in preference to *cōli* which means 'I am going'.)

You May Hear

Feel free to come anytime.
jokhon khushi cōle āsben — যখন খুশি চলে আসবেন

Please come inside.
vitore āsun — ভিতরে আসুন

You don't have to take off your shoes.
jutō khulte hobe nā — জুতো খুলতে হবে না

Please make yourself comfortable.
ārām kōre bōsun — আরাম করে বসুন

Would you like tea or coffee?
cā khāben nā kofi? — চা খাবেন না কফি?

Forms of Address

It is uncommon to address someone simply by name. The equivalent of 'Hello Sir/Madam' or the Bengali address which translates as 'elder brother/sister' are commonly used to address strangers. These forms of address are also used to attract somebody's attention.

Hello Sir/Madam.
sunchen mosāi/didi শুনছেন মশাই / দিদি

Body Language

The words 'yes' and 'no' are indicated by the same gestures as in the West – a nod and a shake of the head. These are the only gestures used by Bengalis. Even winking, nudging or an invitation to shake hands may make people uncomfortable. Physical contact between men and women in public is frowned upon although it is not uncommon to see, especially among younger people.

Small Talk

Bengalis are usually very talkative and are curious about foreigners. Given the chance, they can always be drawn to a conversation. Don't be offended if you are asked what may seem like personal questions. This is just a cultural difference and not a sign of disrespect.

Meeting People

In Bengali there are three forms of the second person pronoun ('you') – formal, familiar and intimate. To be on the safe side, always use the formal address. The following phrases are in this form.

Hello. My name is ... *nomoskār. āmār nām ...*	নমস্কার। আমার নাম ...
What's your name? *āpnār nām ki?*	আপনার নাম কি?
Let me introduce you to ... *poricoy/ālāp kōriye diyee*	পরিচয় / আলাপ করিয়ে দিই
I'm pleased to meet you. *khub vālō lāglō ālāp hōye*	খুব ভাল লাগলো আলাপ হোয়ে
Please visit our hotel some day. *akdin cole āsun āmāder hōṭele*	একদিন চলে আসুন আমাদের হোটেলে

Nationalities

Where (which country) do you come from?
āpni kōthā theke āschen? আপনি কোথা থেকে আসছেন?

I am from ...	*āmi ... theke āschi*	আমি ... থেকে আসছি
Australia	*ostreliā*	অষ্ট্রেলিয়া
East Bengal	*purbo bānglā*	পুর্ব বাংলা
West Bengal	*poscim bongo*	পশ্চিম বঙ্গ
Canada	*kānāḍā*	কানাডা
China	*cinā*	চিনা
France	*frāns*	ফ্রান্স
Germany	*jārmāni*	জার্মানী
Greece	*gris*	গ্রীস
India	*bhārot*	ভারত
Italy	*itāli*	ইটালী
Japan	*jāpān*	জাপান
Russia	*rāsiā*	রাশিয়া
UK	*iunāiṭed kingdum*	ইউনাইটেড কিংডাম
USA	*āmerikā*	আমেরিকা

Age

It is not considered impolite to ask someone their age.

How old are you?
āpnār boyos koto? আপনার বয়স কত ?

I am ... years old.	*āmār boyos ...*	আমার বয়স ...
16	*sōlō*	ষোল
38	*āṭtiris*	আটত্রিশ

(see Numbers & Amounts, page 104, for particular ages)

Occupations

What is your occupation?
āpni ki koren? আপনি কি করেন?

I am a/an ...	*āmi akjon ...*	আমি একজন ...
actor	*obhinetā* (m)	অভিনেতা (m)
	obhinetri (f)	অভিনেত্রী (f)
architect	*sthopoti*	স্থপতি
artist	*silpi*	শিল্পী
business person	*babosāi*	ব্যাবসায়ী
carpenter	*chutōr*	ছুতোর
chemist	*rāsā yonik*	রাসায়নিক
clerk	*kerāni*	কেরানী
doctor	*ḍāktār*	ডাক্তার
engineer	*inginiār*	ইন্‌জিনিয়ার
interpreter	*dobhāsi*	দোভাষী
journalist	*sāngbādik*	সাংবাদিক
lawyer	*ukil*	উকিল
manager	*manejār*	ম্যানেজার
manual worker	*kuli/mojur*	কুলি / মজুর
musician	*bādok*	বাদক
nurse	*nārs*	নার্স
office worker	*ofis cākure*	ওফিস চাকুরে
owner	*mālik*	মালিক
salesperson	*bikreta*	বিক্রেতা
scientist	*biggāni*	বিজ্ঞানী
singer	*gāyāk*	গায়ক
student	*chātro* (m)	ছাত্র (m)
	chātri (f)	ছাত্রী (f)
teacher	*sikkhok* (m)	শিক্ষক (m)
	shikkhikā (f)	শিক্ষিকা (f)

waiter	*beāra*	বেয়ারা
writer	*lekhok* (m)	লেখক (m)
	lekhikā (f)	লেখিকা (f)

Religion

Religion plays an important role in Bengali life. Islam is the religion of the majority of Bangladeshis. More than 80% of the population claim to be Muslim, while Hindus and Buddhists make up most of the remaining 20%. In India Hindu is the major religion while Islam is the largest minority religion, numbering about 10% of the population.

What is your religion?
āpnār dhormo ki? আপনার ধর্ম কি?

I am ...	*āmi ...*	আমি ...
Buddhist	*bōuddō*	বৌদ্ধ
Christian	*khrisṭān*	খ্রিস্টান
Hindu	*hindu*	হিন্দু
Jewish	*pādri*	পাদ্রী
Muslim	*musolmān*	মুসলমান

Bengalis may feel uncomfortable if you do not profess a religion. To avoid any embarrassment, it may be a good idea to claim a religion.

Family

Are you married?
āpni bibāhito? — আপনি বিবাহিত?

No, I am unmarried.
nā, āmi biye korini (m)/ *kumāri* (f) — না আমি বিয়ে করিনি / আমি কুমারী (f)

I am a widow/widower.
āmi bidhobā/bipotnik — আমি বিধবা (f)/ বিপত্নীক (m)

Do you have any children?
āpnār chele-pule āche ki? — আপনার ছেলে পুলে আছে কি?

Yes, I have a son/daughter.
hā̃, āmār ak chele/meye — হ্যাঁ, আমার এক ছেলে / মেয়ে.

I don't have any children.
āmār chele-pule neyi — আমার ছেলে পুলে নেই

How many brothers and sisters do you have?
āpnār bhāi bōn koṭi? — আপনার ভাই বোন কটি?

Is your husband/wife with you?
āpnār swāmi/stri āpnār songe esechen ki? — আপনার স্বামী / স্ত্রী আপনার সংগে এসেছেন কি ?

Are your parents here with you?
āpnār mā-bābā songe āchen? — আপনার মা বাবা সংগে আছেন?

Relations

In Bengali there is an etiquette of direct address. These kinship terms clearly differentiate between relatives who are older or younger, maternal or paternal.

mother	*mā/āmmā* (B)	মা / আম্মা (B)
father	*bābā/ābbā* (B)	বাবা / আব্বা (B)
son	*chele/putro*	ছেলে / পুত্র
daughter	*meye/konyā*	মেয়ে / কন্যা
grandfather	*dādu/nānā* (B)	দাদু / নানা (B)
grandmother	*didā/nāni* (B)	দিদা / নানী (B)
uncle (paternal)	*kākā/cācā* (B)	কাকা / চাচা (B)
uncle (maternal)	*māmā*	মামা
aunt (paternal)	*pisi/fufu* (B)	পিসী / ফুফু (B)
aunt (maternal)	*māsi/khālā* (B)	মাসী / খালা (B)
elder brother	*dādā/bhāijān* (B)	দাদা / ভাইজান (B)
elder sister	*didi/āppā* (B)	দিদি / আপা (B)
younger brother	*bhāi/bhāiā* (B)	ভাই / ভাইয়া (B)
younger sister	*bōn*	বোন
baby	*shishu/bāccā*	শিশু / বাচ্চা
grandson/granddaughter	*nāti/nātni*	নাতি (m)/ নাতনী (f)
family	*pōribār*	পরিবার

These terms are also often used when addressing other people. A young person will address a much older man or woman as *dādu* (grandfather) or *didā* (grandmother). An older but not elderly person will be addressed as *kākā* (uncle) or *pisi* (aunt). Someone roughly the same age but a little older will be addressed as *dādā* (elder brother) or *didi* (elder sister).

The status of relatives is considered important and these terms of address are used with care. The following prefixes are used to denote comparative relations:

elder	*boro-*	বড়
younger	*chōṭō-*	ছোট
middle	*mejō-*	মেজো
step	*sot-*	সৎ

Feelings

Feelings are expressed by nouns used with verbs, not with adjectives as in English.

I am ...	*āmār ...*	আমার ...
angry	*rāg hocche* (lit: I am developing anger)	রাগ হচ্ছে
cold	*sit korche* (lit: I am feeling cold)	শীত করছে
happy	*ānondo hocche*	আনন্দ হচ্ছে
hot	*gorom lāgche*	গরম লাগছে
hungry	*kshide lāgche*	ক্ষিদে লাগছে
in a hurry	*tāṛā āche*	তাড়া আছে
sleepy	*ghum pācche*	ঘুম পাচ্ছে

thirsty	*teṣṭā pācche*	তেষ্টা পাচ্ছে
tired	*klānto lāgche*	ক্লান্ত লাগছে

I am sorry.
dukkhito দুখিঃত
I am thankful/grateful.
dhonyobād ধন্যবাদ

Opinions

Bengalis are quite forthcoming in their opinions and will often express them with conviction.

I agree.
āmār ō tāi mot আমার ও তাই মত
I don't agree.
āmār mot neyi আমার মত নেই
I (don't) know.
āmi jāni (nā) আমি জানি (না)
What do you think?
āpnār ki mot? আপনার কি মত?
I love/like Bengali songs.
āmi bānglā gān bhālobāsi/pochondo kori আমি বাংলা গান ভালবাসি / পছন্দ করি
That's interesting.
āscorjyo আশ্চর্য!
That's beautiful.
sundor/comotkār সুন্দর / চমৎকার!
Really/Truly?
sotyi? সত্যি!
Alright/OK.
ācchā আচ্ছা
Well/Good!
bhālō! ভালো

Language Problems

I don't speak Bengali.
āmi bānglā jāni nā — আমি বাংলা জানিনা
(lit: I Bengali don't know)

I am a foreigner.
āmi bideshii — আমি বিদেশী

Is there anyone here who speaks English?
ekhāne keu ingrāji jānen ki? — এখানে কেউ ইংরাজী জানেন কি?

I (don't) understand.
bujhte pārlām (nā) — বুঝতে পারলাম না

Please speak slowly.
āste bōlben ki? — আস্তে বলবেন কি?

How do you say it in Bengali?
eke bānglāy ki bole? — একে বাংলায় কি বলে?

I know a few words of Bengali.
āmi ekṭu adhṭu bānglā jāni — আমি একটু আধটু বাংলা জানি

Some Useful Phrases

Yes.	*hā̃*	হাঁ
No.	*nā*	না
Please.	*doyā kōre*	দয়া করে
Thank you.	*dhonyobād*	ধন্যবাদ
OK.	*ācchā*	আচ্ছা
Sure.	*niscoy*	নিশ্চয়
Maybe/Perhaps.	*hoyto*	হয়ত
What a lovely day!	*ājker dinṭā ki sundor!*	আজকের দিনটা কি সুন্দর!

SMALL TALK

Amazing!	*odvut!*	অদ্ভুত !
Beautiful!	*opurbo/sundor/ comotkār!*	অপূর্ব / সুন্দর / চমৎকার !
What is this/that?	*eṭā ki?*	এটা কি ?
Is it OK?	*ṭhik āche?*	ঠিক আছে ?
So-so.	*ak-rokom*	একরকম
No problem	*hōye jābe* (lit: it will be done)	হয়ে যাবে

Never mind/It doesn't matter.
ō kichu noy ও কিছু নয়

Are you on holiday?
āpni ki chuṭite āchen? আপনি কি ছুটিতে আছেন ?

Do you live here?
āpni ki ekhāne thāken? আপনি কি এখানে থাকেন ?

Do you like it here?
ekhāne āpnār vālō lāge? এখানে আপনার ভালো লাগে ?

Yes, a lot.
khub খুব

Please wait here.
ekhāne opekshā korun এখানে অপেক্ষা করুন

Please don't smoke.
dhumpan korben nā ধুমপান করবেন না

Getting Around

West Bengal is a crowded place and getting from one place to another can be exhausting. There are not many signs to direct travellers although you will find that people are very helpful in giving directions. English words are used in connection with most forms of transport.

If you are using public transport get hold of a city map, although you may have difficulty finding an up-to-date one. Lonely Planet's *India: travel survival kit* and *Bangladesh: travel survival kit* include accurate street maps showing public transport routes and stops in Calcutta, Darjeeling and Dhaka. Always take the card of your hotel with you and, if lost, take a taxi.

Finding Your Way

Most destination names in Bengali are used unaltered from English.

Where is the ...?	*... kōthāyo bōlben ki?*	... কোথায় বলুন ত?
How far is the ...?	*... koto dur?*	... কত দুর?
station	*sṭeson*	ষ্টেশান
airport	*eārpōrṭ*	এয়ারপোর্ট
bus stop	*bās sṭop*	বাসস্টপ
tram stop	*trām sṭop*	ট্রামস্টপ
taxi stand	*ṭaksi sṭanḍ*	ট্যাক্সি ষ্ট্যান্ড

hotel	*hōṭel*	হোটেল
post office	*ḍāk ghor*	ডাকঘর

Can I walk there?
h̃eṭe jāyōā jābe ki? — হেঁটে যাওয়া যাবে কি ?
(lit: do you think I can walk up to there?)

How do I get to ...?
... ki kōre jāi bōlun tō? — ... কি করে যাই বলুন ত?

What time does the ... leave/arrive?	*... kokhon chāṛbe/ p̃ōuchōbe?*	... কখন ছাড়বে / পোঁছোবে?
bus	*bās*	বাস
train	*tren*	ট্রেন
tram	*ṭrām*	ট্রাম

Directions

north	*uttor*	উত্তর
south	*dokkhin*	দক্ষিণ
east	*purbo*	পূর্ব্ব
west	*poscim*	পশ্চিম
right	*ḍāine*	ডাইনে
left	*b̃āye*	বাঁয়ে
in front	*sāmne*	সামনে
behind	*pechone*	পেছনে
up	*upore*	উপরে
down	*niice*	নীচে
opposite	*ulṭō*	উল্টো
across	*ōpār*	ওপার
direction	*dik*	দিক

Buying Tickets

Where is the ticket office?
ṭikiṭ ofis kōthāy? — টিকিট অফিস কোথায়?

How much is the fare to ...?
... jete koto bhāṛā lāgbe? — ... যেতে কত ভাড়া লাগবে?

I'd like ... ticket(s) to ..., please.	*āmi ... ... ṭikiṭ cāi*	আমি ... টিকিট চাই
one	*ekṭa*	একটা
two	*duṭō*	দুটো
one-way	*ek-diker*	একদিককার
return	*du-diker/āsā jāōār*	দুদিকের / আসা-যাওয়ার
1st class	*fārsṭ klās*	ফার্স্ট ক্লাস
economy	*sostar*	সস্তার।

Air

Is there a flight to ...?
... plen jāyo ki? — ... প্লেন যায় কি?

When is the next flight to ...?
... jāōār plen kokhon? — ... যাওয়ার প্লেন কখন?

How long does the flight to ... take?
... jete plene koto-kkhon lāge? — ... যেতে প্লেনে কতক্ষন লাগে?

Where do we check in?
kōthāy cek-in? — কোথায় চেক-ইন?

I would like to buy a ticket to ...
akṭā ...-r ṭikiṭ din — একটা ... র টিকিট দিন

cancel	*nākoc/bātil*	নাকচ / বাতিল
departure	*chāṛār*	ছাড়ার

arrival	*āsār*	আসার
delay	*derii/bilombo*	দেরী / বিলম্ব

Bus & Tram

Trams run in some cities. Buses are available in towns and are often the only available transport to the more remote places.

Which bus/tram do I catch for ...?
... jete kōn bās/ṭrām dhōrbō bōlun to? ... যেতে কোন বাস / ট্রাম ধরব বলুন ত?

When is the ... bus/tram?	*... bās/trām kokhon chārbe?*	... বাস / ট্রাম কখন ছাড়বে?
next	*porer*	পরের
first	*prothom*	প্রথম
last	*sesh*	শেষ

What is this place called?
e jāyogār nām ki? এ জায়গার নাম কি ?

Please let me know when it is my stop.
āmār sṭop ele bōlben kintu আমার ষ্টপ এলে বলবেন কিন্তু?

I want to get off here.
āmi ekhāne nāmbo আমি এখানে নামব

Taxi

If you take a taxi, be careful that you are not taken on a joy ride – try to get an idea of what the fare may be before you go. It is always better to take a taxi if travelling at night. Taxis are available only in the major cities. The meters in some taxis are not adjusted to the latest increase due to inflation, so taxi drivers often carry a chart showing the extra fare they can charge. It is not always easy to find a taxi when you need one, so allow plenty of time to catch one, or ask your hotel to order one for you.

Can you call a taxi for me please?
āmār jonyo akṭā ṭaksi ḍeke deben? আমার জন্য একটা ট্যাক্সি ডেকে দেবেন?

Let's go!
colun! চলুন
Please stop here.
ekhāne thāmun এখানে থামুন
Wait for me here.
ekhāne opekkhā korun এখানে অপেক্ষা করুন
I will be back soon.
akhoni āschi এখনি আসছি
What do I owe you?
koto bhāṛā hōlō? কত ভাড়া হল?

Instructions

Turn left/right.
b̃āye/ḍāine ghurun বাঁয়ে / ডাইনে ঘুরুন
Go straight ahead.
sāmne cholun সামনে চলুন
Go to the opposite footpath.
ulṭō fuṭpāthe colun উল্টো ফুটপাথে চলুন
Please hurry.
tāṛātāṛi তাড়াতাড়ি
Slow down.
āste colun আস্তে চলুন

Train

Trains are the cheapest way to travel in Bengal and the train journey is reasonably comfortable. English words are almost always used in connection with a train journey. For example: station, ticket, signal, reservation, 1st/economy/3rd class, platform, ticket office, timetable are all used in Bengali.

Which train goes to ...?
kōn ṭrenṭā ... jābe কোন ট্রেনটা ... যাবে?

Do I have to change?
āmāke ki bodlāte hobe? আমাকে কি বদলাতে হবে?
What is the next station?
er pore kon sṭeson এর পরে কোন ষ্টেশন?

Boat

There are a number of interesting river trips in West Bengal and Bangladesh and numerous ferries across the rivers. Nevertheless, boat journeys can be dangerous and you should scrutinise the weather forecasts before contemplating a journey by boat.

boat	*noukā*	নৌকা
ferry	*kheyā*	খেয়া

Bicycle & Car

Bicycles are not generally used in crowded cities but they are a great way to get around in the country areas and in small towns. Not all towns have facilities for hiring bikes, however. If you want to hire a car, it is better to hire a chauffer as well. Driving can be hazardous and car insurance claims are lengthy to process.

Where can I hire a bicycle/car?
ekhāne kōthāy sāikel/gāṛi bhāṛā pāōa jāyo? এখানে কোথায় সাইকেল / গাড়ী ভাড়া পাওয়া যায়?
How much is the rental/deposit?
bhāṛā/ogrim koto lāgbe? ভাড়া / অগ্রিম কত লাগবে?
I will return it tomorrow.
kāl ferot debo কাল ফেরত দেব
Is insurance included?
biimā kora āche tō? বীমা করা আছে কি?

My car/bicycle has broken down.
āmār gāṛi/sāikel khārāp hōye giyeche — আমার গাড়ী / সাইকেল খারাপ হয়ে গিয়েছে

Where is the nearest petrol station?
kōthāy petrōl pābō? — কোথায় পেট্রোল পাবো ?

Some Useful Words

air	*hāōyā*	হাওয়া
brakes	*brek*	ব্রেক
lane	*gōli*	গলি
lights	*bāti*	বাতি
oil	*tel*	তেল
puncture	*fuṭō*	ফুটো
radiator	*reḍieṭār*	রেডিয়েটার
road	*rāstā*	রাস্তা
tyre	*ṭāiār*	টায়ার

Other Transport

There are other forms of transport in Bengal such as rickshaws and scooter-taxis. The latter sometimes have meters. If there is no meter, the drivers may charge as they wish. It is better to agree on a fare before the commencement of the journey. During peak hours taxis and scooter-taxis have a sharing arrangement which is cheap and convenient.

Bargaining

Bargaining is very common in Bengal. If you feel uneasy bargaining you may end up paying more than you should. Enquire at your hotel or from friends about reasonable fares.

That's too expensive.
boḍḍo besi cāichen — বড্ড বেশী চাইছেন

I will pay ...
... debo — ... দেব

Accommodation

Accommodation varies from expensive hotels to basic guest-houses with next-to-nothing rates. Rates vary drastically from one place to another and bargaining in this situation is quite common.

Can you recommend a ... hotel/ guesthouse?	*akṭā ... hōtel er k͠hōj dite pāren?*	একটা ... হোটেলের খোঁজ দিতে পারেন?
good	*bhālō*	ভাল
cheap	*sostār*	সস্তার
nearby	*kāchākāchi*	কাছাকাছি

At the Hotel

Not all hotels offer the standard facilities. Hot and cold running water, a room refrigerator and air-conditioning and heating may not necessarily be available.

Checking In

Do you have any rooms available?
āpnāder kōnō ghor khāli āche ki? আপনাদের কোন ঘর খালি আছে কি?

I would like a ... room.	*āmi akṭā ... ghor cāi*	আমি একটা ... ঘর চাই
single	*singl/ekā thākār*	সিঙ্গল / একা থাকার
double	*dobl/dujon thākār*	ডবল / দুজন থাকার
road-facing	*rāstār diker*	রাস্তার দিকের
Does the room have ...?	*ghore ... āche ki?*	ঘরে ... আছে কি?
a bathroom	*lāgoā bāthrum*	লাগোয়া বাথরুম
hot water	*gorom jol*	গরম জল
a telephone	*ṭelifōn*	টেলিফোন

What is the cost per night?
bhāṛā koto? ভাড়া কত?

Do you have a student discount?
chātroder jonyo kōnō subidhā āche ki? ছাত্রদের জন্য কোন সুবিধা আছে কি?

Can I see the room?
ghor dekhte pāri? ঘর দেখতে পারি?

Are there any other rooms?
ār kōnō ghor āche ki? আর কোন ঘর আছে কি?
Is there a cheaper one?
sostār kōnō ghor āche ki? সস্তার কোন ঘর আছে কি?
It's fine. I'll take it.
ṭhik āche. eṭāi nebo ঠিক আছে। এটাই নেব
I am not sure how long I'll be staying.
kotodin thākbo ṭhik neyi কতদিন থাকবো ঠিক নেই

I'm staying for ...	*āmi ... thākbo*	আমি ... থাকবো
one night	*ak rāt*	এক রাত
one week	*ak soptāho*	এক সপ্তাহ

I would like to have the key please.
ghorer cābi din ঘরের চাবি দিন
Can someone take my luggage to my room?
kāuke bōlben āmār māl upōre niye jete? কাউকে বলবেন আমার মাল উপরে নিয়ে যেতে ?

Requests & Complaints

I don't like this room.
e ghor pochondo noy এ ঘব পছন্দ নয়

It's too ...	*ghor khub ...*	ঘর খুব ...
cold	*ṭhānḍā*	ঠান্ডা
hot	*gorom*	গরম
big	*boṛo*	বড়
small	*choṭō*	ছোট
dark	*ondhokār*	অন্ধকার

The ... in my room does not work. — *āmār ghorer ... khārāp hoye gache* — আমার ঘরের ... খারাপ হয়ে গেছে

- light — *bāti* — বাতি
- tap — *joler kol* — জলের কল

Can you get it repaired?
oṭā sāriye debār babostā kōrben ki?
ওটা সারিয়ে দেবার ব্যাবস্থা করবেন কি ?

I would like to change to another room.
āmi ghor bodlāte cāi
আমি ঘর বদলাতে চাই

The room needs to be cleaned.
ghor poriskār kore din
ঘর পরিস্কার করে দিন

Please change the sheets.
cādor bōdle din
চাদর বদলে দিন

Can you please wake me up at 6.30 am tomorrow?
kāl sokāl sāṛe choṭāyo tule deben ki?
কাল সকাল সাড়ে ছটায় তুলে দেবেন কি?

Checking Out

We would like to check out ...	*āmrā ... ghor chere debo*	আমরা ... ঘর ছেড়ে দেব
at noon today	*āj dupure*	আজ দুপুরে
now	*ekhuni*	এখুনি
tomorrow	*kāl*	কাল

Please prepare my bill.
āmār hisābṭā din আমার হিসাবটা দিন

I am returning ...	*āmi ... firbo*	আমি ... ফিরব
tomorrow	*kāl*	কাল
day after tomorrow	*porshu*	পরশু
in a few days	*kichu din pore*	কিছুদিন পরে

Can I leave my bags here?
āmār mālpotro ekhāne rekhe jete pari? আমার মালপত্র এখানে রেখে যেতে পারি?

Laundry

Larger hotels have laundrettes and dry-cleaning services. If not, they will recommend a laundry service nearby.

Is there a ... service?	*ekhāne jāmākāpor ... babostā āche ki?*	এখানে জামাকাপড় ... ব্যাবস্থা আছে কি?
laundry	*kācār*	কাচার
ironing	*istrir*	ইস্ত্রির

When will they be ready?
kokhon ferot pābo? কখন ফেরত পাব?

I need them today/tomorrow.
āj/kāl ferot cāi — আজ / কাল ফেরত চাই

Is my laundry ready?
āmār kāpoṛ kācā hoye eseche ki? — আমার কাপড়কাচা হয়ে এসেছে কি?

These are not mine.
egulō āmār noy — এগুলো আমার নয়

There's a shirt missing.
akṭā jāmā kom — একটা জামা কম

Some Useful Words

address	*ṭhikānā*	ঠিকানা
air-conditioning	*sito-tāp niyontrito*	শীততাপ নিয়ন্ত্রিত

bed	*bichānā*	বিছানা
blanket	*kombol*	কম্বল
bucket	*bālti*	বালতি
candle	*mombāti*	মোমবাতি
clean	*poriskār*	পরিস্কার
cot	*khāṭ*	খাট
dirty	*moylā*	ময়লা
fan	*pākhā*	পাখা
heating	*uttāp*	উত্তাপ
key	*cābi*	চাবি
lock	*tālā*	তালা
mat	*mādur*	মাদুর
mattress	*tōsok*	তোষক
mirror	*āynā*	আয়না
pillow	*bālish*	বালিশ
plug	*ilekṭrik plāg*	ইলেকট্রিক প্লাগ্
quiet	*nijhum*	নিঝুম
quilt	*lep*	লেপ
sheet	*cādor*	চাদর
soap	*sābān*	সাবান
toilet	*pāykhānā*	পায়খানা
toilet paper	*pāykhānār kagoj*	পায়খানার কাগজ
(hot/cold) water	*(gorom/ṭhāndā) jol/pāni* (B)	(গরম ঠান্ডা) জল / পানি
window	*jānālā*	জানালা

Around Town

Both Dhaka (the capital of Bangladesh) and Calcutta (the capital of West Bengal) are very crowded cities. You will notice an interesting blend of modern and ancient buildings and sights. Public transport moves at a very leisurely pace, as there is always a great deal of traffic. Many people in Dhaka prefer to travel in rickshaws than in crowded buses or trains. There are no autorickshaws in the CBD of Calcutta, however, and taxis are difficult to get. Allow plenty of time for travel within the cities.

How do I get to the ...?	*... ki kōre jāi bōlun tō?*	... কি করে যাই বলুন ত?
Where is the ...?	*... kōthāy?*	... কোথায়?
bank	*bank*	ব্যাঙ্ক
... embassy	*... dutābās*	... দুতাবাস
hospital	*hāspātāl*	হাসপাতাল
hotel	*hōṭel*	হোটেল
market	*bājār*	বাজার
mosque	*mosjid*	মসজিদ
museum	*jādughor*	যাদুঘর
palace	*prāsād*	প্রাসাদ
park	*bāgān/moydān*	বাগান / ময়দান
police station	*thānā*	থানা
post office	*pōsṭāfis/dākghor*	পোষ্টাফিস / ডাকঘর

public toilet	*sōucāgār* (S)	শৌচাগার
tourist office	*porjyoṭon ofis* (S)	পর্যটন অফিস
university	*biswobidyāloy* (S)	বিশ্ববিদ্যালয়

At the Bank

The currency in West Bengal and in Bangladesh is rupees or *taka*, although the exchange rates are different. US dollars are more easily converted than any other currency. There is a rampant black market that offers attractive exchange rates. You can convert any extra local money at the airport if you show official receipts. Local banks are not fully computerised so expect delays in transactions. It is advisable to deal with a foreign bank if there is one.

I want to exchange a travellers' cheque.
āmi ṭrāvelār cek bhāngāte cāi — আমি ট্রাভেলার চেক ভাঙ্গাতে চাই

Can I change this into rupees?
egulō ṭākāy bhāngāte pāri? এগুলো টাকায় ভাঙ্গাতে পারি?

What is the exchange rate today?
ājker excenj ret ki? আজকের এক্সচেঞ্জ রেট কি?

Can you cash a personal cheque?
āmār nāmer akṭā cek bhāngānō jābe ki? আমার নামের একটা চেক ভাঙ্গানো যাবে কি?

I am expecting some money from abroad.
bidesh theke āmār nāme kichu ṭākā āsār kothā āche বিদেশ থেকে আমার নামে কিছু টাকা আসার কথা আছে

Can you please give me some change from this 100-rupee note?
eyi aksho ṭakār khucro deben ki? এই একশ টাকার খুচরো দেবেন কি ?

At the Post Office

Where is the post office?
ḍākghor kothay bōlte pāren? ডাকঘর কোথায় বোলতে পারবেন?

How much does it cost to send a ... to Canada?	*akṭā ... kānāḍā pāṭhāte koto lāgbe?*	একটা ... কানাডা পাঠাতে কত লাগবে?
envelope	*khām*	খাম
letter	*ciṭhi*	চিঠি
parcel	*pārsel/taṛā*	পার্শেল / তাড়া
postcard	*posṭ kāṛ*	পোষ্টকার্ড

I want to send a telegram to ...
āmi ... akṭā ṭeligrām pāṭhāte cāi — আমি ... একটা টেলিগ্রাম পাঠাতে চাই

address	*ṭhikānā*	ঠিকানা
express mail	*ekspres mele*	এক্সপ্রেস মেলে
registered mail	*registry kōre*	রেজিষ্ট্রি করে
stamp	*dāk ṭikiṭ*	ডাক টিকিট

Telephone & Fax

Facilities for both telephone and fax are now available in public booths and in the post office in major cities. Service is quick, direct and reliable.

How much is it to send a fax to ...?
akṭā fax ... pāṭhāte koto khoroc? — একটা ফ্যাক্স ... পাঠাতে কত খরচ?

I'd like to make a (reverse charges/collect) call to ...
āmi aktā revārs cārge kol kōrte cāi ... — আমি একটা রিভার্স চার্জ কল করতে চাই

How much is the call per minute to ...?
... fōn kōrte miniṭe koto khoroc? — ... ফোন করতে মিনিটে কত খরচ?

We were cut off.
lāin ke ṭe geche — লাইন কেটে গেছে

Please say that I rang.
bolben āmi fōn kōrechilām — বলবেন আমি ফোন করেছিলাম

I'll call again at ...
ābār ... ṭāy fōn kōrbo — আবার ... টায় ফোন করব

At the Zoo

Does this zoo keep tigers in cages?
eyi ciṛiākhānāyo bāgh ki k̃hācāyo thāke? — এই চিড়িয়াখানায় বাঘ কি খাঁচায় থাকে?

Beware! The monkey may snatch food from you.
sābdhān! b̃ādore khābār keṛe nebe — সাবধান, বাঁদরে খাবার কেড়ে নেবে!

These snakes are poisonous.
sāpgulō bisākto — সাপগুলো বিষাক্ত

(See page 66 for a list of animals)

Entertainment

Most places do not have much nightlife. Larger towns have bars in major hotels, some of them may even have discos. But there is no dearth of entertainment. There are plenty of cinemas, theatres, concerts and shows. Bengal is very rich in its cultural heritage and you will find music or other festivals all the year round.

Where can I see a music performance?
kōthāy jolsā dekte pāri? — কোথায় জলসা দেখতে পারি?

What kind of festival is this?
e kiser utsob? — এ কিসের উৎসব?

What kind of music will be performed in this festival?
eṭā ki dhoroner gāner utsob? — এটা কি ধরনের গানের উৎসব?

What's on at the cinema/theatre?
ki ki sinemā/thieṭār cōlche? কি কি সিনেমা / থিয়েটার চলছে?

What language is it in?
eyi sinemā kōn bhāsāyo? এই সিনেমা কোন ভাষায়?

How much is a ticket?
ṭikiṭer dām kotō? টিকিটের দাম কত?

Sightseeing

There are organised tours in every major town. Check with your hotel or tourist information office.

Where can I get a local map?
ekhānkār māncitro kothāyo pābō bōlun to? এখানকার মানচিত্র কোথায় পাবো বলুন ত?

When does ... open/close?
... kokhon khōle/bondho hoi ? ... কখন খোলে / বন্ধ হয়?

What's that building?
ōi bāṛi ṭā kiser? — এই বাড়িটা কিসের?

Is this ancient?
eṭā ki khub prācin? — এটা কি খুব প্রাচীন?

Who lived here?
ekhāne ke thākto? — এখানে কে থাকতো?

How much is the entry fee?
ḍhukte kotō lāgbe? — ঢুকতে কত লাগবে?

Do you have a student discount?
chātrader kōnō subidhe āche? — ছাত্রদের কোন সুবিধা আছে?

May I take a photo?
ekhāne foṭō tulte pāri? — এখানে ফটো তুলতে পারি?

Places to See In Dhaka

Shonar Gaon — সমীবা আশ্রম
Samiba Ashram — ধানমন্ডি
Dhamondi — সোনার গাঁও

Places to See In & Around Calcutta

India Museum	যাদুঘর
Bidhan Setu	বিধান সেতু
Rabindra Sarobar	রবীন্দ্র সরোবর
Patal Rail	পাতাল রেল
Shanti Niketan	শান্তিনিকেতন
Belur	বেলুড়
Kali Temple	কালীমন্দির
Sagar Mela	সাগর মেলা
Digha	দীঘা
Haldia	হলদিয়া
Nakhoda Mosque	নাখোদা মসজিদ
Rabindra Sadan	রবীন্দ্র সদন

Signs

Almost all signs are in English with the exception of 'Toilets' which is often written in Bengali.

শৌচাগার (মহিলা / পুরুষ)	TOILETS (MEN'S/WOMEN'S)

Paperwork

If you have to deal with any government office, make sure you allow plenty of time. If there is no embassy or consulate locally, seek advice from your hotel.

first name	*prothom nām*	প্রথম নাম
surname	*gōṭro nām/podobii*	গোত্র নাম / পদবী
address	*ṭhikānā*	ঠিকানা

age	*boyos*	বয়স
sex	*lingo*	লিঙ্গ
religion	*dhormo*	ধর্ম
occupation/ profession	*cākri*	চাকরি
passport no.	*pāspōter nombōr*	পাসপোর্ট নম্বর
driving licence	*drāiving lāisens*	ড্রাইভিং লাইসেন্স

Police

I want to report a lost ...
āmār ... hāriyeche. ḍāyeri kōrte cāi — আমার ... হারিয়েছে। ডায়েরী করতে চাই

My ... has been stolen from the hotel.
hōṭel theke āmār ... curi giyeche — হোটেল থেকে আমার ... চুরি গিয়েছে

I am lost.
āmi poth hāriyechi — আমি পথ হারিয়েছি

I have no money.
āmār kāche ṭākākoṛi neyi — আমার কাছে টাকাকড়ি নেই

Can you help me find ... hotel?
āmāke ... hoṭele pōuche deben? — আমাকে ... হোটেলে পৌঁছে দেবেন?

In the Country

There is very little transport in the remote villages in Bengal so many of these places are virtually inaccessible to travellers. There are also beautiful country towns in both West Bengal and Bangladesh where life is much more pleasant than in the cities. They are well serviced by transport from the capital cities. You can get a list of these places and what they have to offer from your travel agent or from your hotel.

Is there any transport to ...?
... grāme jāōār kōnō jān bāhon āche ki? গ্রামে যাওয়ার কোন যানবাহন আছে কি?

Is there a ferry that crosses this river?
ōyi nodi pār hōār kōnō kheyā āche ki? এই নদী পার হওয়ার কোন খেয়া আছে কি?

Are there any boats for hire?
noukā bhāṛā pāōā jābe ki? নৌকা ভাড়া পাওয়া যাবে কি?

Can we get a taxi or a rickshaw to go to ...?
... jete kōnō gāṛi bā riksā pāōā jābe ki? যেতে কোন গাড়ী বা রিক্সা পাওয়া যাবে কি?

Weather

What will the weather be like today?
āj ābhāōyā kamon? আজ আবহাওয়া কেমন?

The weather will be ...	*ājker ābhāōyā... hobe*	আজকের আবহাওয়া ... হবে
cloudy	*meghlā*	মেঘলা
nice	*sundor*	সুন্দর
humid	*vapsā*	ভ্যাপসা
hot	*gorom*	গরম
cold	*ṭhānḍā*	ঠান্ডা

It may rain/be stormy today.
āj brisṭi/jhoṛ hobe আজ বৃষ্টি ঝড় হবে

It may snow today.
āj borof pōṛte pāre আজ বরফ পড়তে পারে

Trekking

The Himalayan mountain range cuts right across Bengal. There are some very picturesque spots in this part of the Himalayas. The Himalayan Mountaineering Institute, founded by Tenjing Norke (the first person to reach Everest along with Edmund Hillary) is in Darjeeling. You will find many established trekking routes in this area.

Hiring Porters

Will you come with me?	
āpni āmār songe āsben?	আপনি আমার সঙ্গে আসবেন?
I am going to ...	
āmi ... jācchi	আমি ... যাচ্ছি
How many days will it take?	
koto din lāgbe?	কতদিন লাগবে?
What do you charge per day?	
ak diner jonyo koto neben?	একদিনের জন্য কত নেবেন?
How much for the horse/mule?	
ghōṛā/khocchor-er bhāṛā koto?	ঘোড়া / খচ্চরের ভাড়া কত?

Does your rate include ...?	*āpnār bhāṛā ki ... suddho?*	আপনার ভাড়া কি ... শুদ্ধ?
food	*khābār*	খাবার
load	*māl*	মাল

backpack	*bōjhā*	বোঝা
compass	*kompās*	কম্পাস
matches	*diāsālāyi*	দিয়াশালাই
penknife	*churi*	ছুরি
rope	*doṛi*	দড়ি
tent	*t̃ābu*	তাঁবু
tent poles	*k̃huṭi*	খুঁটি
torch	*mosāl*	মশাল

Animals

animal	*jontu/poshu/jānōyār*	জন্তু / প শু / জানোয়ার
buffalo	*mōhish*	মহিষ
camel	*uṭ*	উট
cat	*beṛāl*	বেড়াল
cow	*goru* (m)/*gāi* (f)	গরু (m)/ গাই (f)
crocodile	*kumiir*	কুমীর
deer	*hōrin*	হরিণ
dog	*kukur*	কুকুর
donkey	*gādhā*	গাধা
fish	*māch*	মাছ
frog	*bang*	ব্যাঙ
goat	*chāgol*	ছাগল
horse	*ghōṛā*	ঘোড়া
monkey	*b̃ādor*	বাঁদর
mouse	*ĩdur*	ইঁদুর

ox	*s̃hāṛ*	ষাঁড়
pig	*suyōr*	শূয়োর
rabbit	*khorgōs*	খরগোস
rat	*ĩdur*	ইঁদুর
sheep	*vaṛā*	ভেড়া
snake	*sāp*	সাপ
spider	*mākoṛshā*	মাকড়সা
squirrel	*kāṭhberālii*	কাঠবেড়ালী
turtle	*kocchop*	কচ্ছপ

tiger
bāgh
বাঘ

Insects

ant	*p̃ipṛe*	পিঁপড়ে
butterfly	*projāpoti*	প্রজাপতি
cockroach	*ārshōlā*	আরশোলা
fly	*māchi*	মাছি
insect	*pōkā*	পোকা
leech	*j̃ōk*	জোঁক
lice	*ukun*	উকুন
mosquito	*moshā*	মশা

Birds

bird	*pākhii*	পাখী
chicken	*murgii*	মুরগী
crow	*kāk*	কাক
cuckoo	*kōkil*	কোকিল
duck	*pātihās*	পাতিহাঁস
dove	*ghughu*	ঘুঘু
goose	*hās*	হাঁস
hawk	*bājpākhii*	বাজপাখী
parrot	*ṭiyā*	টিয়া
peacock	*moyuur*	ময়ূর
pigeon	*pāyrā*	পায়রা
rooster	*mōrōg*	মোরগ
sparrow	*coṛuyi*	চড়ুই

Plants

bamboo	*bāsh*	বাঁশ
branch	*ḍāl*	ডাল
creeper	*lotā*	লতা
flower	*ful*	ফুল
fruit	*fol*	ফল
grass	*ghās*	ঘাস
leaf	*pātā*	পাতা
lily	*shāluk*	শালুক
lotus	*podmo*	পদ্ম
palm tree	*tāl gāch*	তালগাছ
sugar cane	*ākh*	আঁখ
tree	*gāch*	গাছ
wood	*kāṭh*	কাঠ

Geographical Terms

beach	*somudro tiir*	সমুদ্র তীর
bridge	*pul/setu*	পুল / সেতু
cave	*guhā*	গুহা
city	*sohor/nogor*	সহর / নগর
field	*māṭh*	মাঠ
forest/jungle	*b̃ādāṛ/jongol*	বন / জঙ্গল
harbour/port	*bondor*	বন্দর
hill	*pāhāṛ*	পাহাড়
hot spring	*ushno prosrobon*	উষ্ম প্রস্রবণ
island	*dwiip*	দ্বীপ
lake	*hrod*	হ্রদ
map	*māncitro*	মানচিত্র
mountain (range)	*porbot (mālā)*	পর্ব্বত (মালা)
ocean	*somudro*	সমুদ্র
pond	*pukur/ḍōbā*	পুকুর / ডোবা
river	*nodii*	নদী
valley	*upotyokā*	উপত্যকা
waterfall	*jolopropāt*	জলপ্রপাত

Food

Indian food is well known for its aroma and spice content – Bengali food is no exception. There is a great variety of delicious fish dishes and Bengalis are renowned for their delicious milk-based sweets. Main meals always include rice, which is cooked in various ways, eg boiled, fried, flaked or bubbled. There are normally four meals per day; the midday meal and dinner being the largest. Many Bengalis are vegetarian, which may mean no fish or eggs, or even onions and garlic. Non-vegetarian Hindus can't eat beef and Muslims can't eat pork.

Delicious!	*suswādu!*	সুস্বাদু
food	*khābār*	খাবার
eat/drink/smoke	*khāōyā*	খাওয়া

(There is one verb for all these actions as they are all taken by the mouth.)

Etiquette

It is customary to use your fingers to eat. In the country it is not uncommon to sit on a rug on the floor, where the meal is served on a banana leaf or some other leaf. Generally, alcohol is not served at a private house. Meals are usually finished off with a dessert *(misṭi)*, usually milk-based, and some spice or beetle leaf. Bengalis make very generous hosts and you are likely to be served large helpings.

At the Restaurant

Even though there are all kinds of restaurants in the major cities, you will be lucky to find one that serves typical Bengali dishes. You will have better luck in hotels. Menus are usually written in English and you shouldn't have any trouble finding an English-speaking waiter to explain any particular dish.

We need a table for two.
dujon bosār tebil cāi — দুজন বসার টেবিল চাই

Do you have a menu in English?
ingrājite lekhā menu āche ki? — ইংরাজিতে লেখা মেনু আছে কি?

I am vegetarian.
āmi nirāmishāshi — আমি নিরামিষাশী

I can't eat ...	*āmi ... khete pārinā*	আমি ... খেতে পারিনা
beef	*gōmāngso*	গোমাংস
chilli	*jhāl*	ঝাল
fish	*māch*	মাছ

I'll have a little ...
āmi ekṭukhāni ... khābo — আমি একটুখানি ...খাব

What is in this dish?
eyi torkāri-te ki ki āche? — এই তরকারিতে কি কি আছে?

What is your best fish dish?
sobceye bhālo mācher torkāri ki? — সবচেয়ে ভাল মাছের তরকারি কি?

I/We would like ...
āmār/āmāder ... pochondo — আমার / আমাদের ... পছন্দ

Making desserts

Is there a dessert which is a speciality of this place?
ekhānkār bikhyāto misṭi ki? এখানকার বিখ্যাত মিষ্টি কি?

May I have the bill?
āmār hisābṭā deben? আমার হিসাবটা দেবেন?

dish	*torkāri*	তরকারি
knife	*churi*	ছুরি
fork	*k̃āṭā*	কাঁটা
spoon	*cāmoc*	চামচ
glass	*glās*	গ্লাস
menu	*menu*	মেনু
napkin/serviette	*rumāl*	রুমাল

FOOD

Speciality Dishes

pāyes পায়েস
a sweet dish usually saucy, eg rice or semolina pudding

cāṭni চাটনি
sweet and sour dish made with mango or lemon, etc

torkāri তরকারি
a general term that refers to any side dish
ḍāl ডাল
lentil soup
pōlāō পোলাও
fried rice
māngser/mācher jhōl মাংসের / মাছের ঝোল
meat/fish curry
k̃hicuṛi খিঁচু ড়ি
a mixed meal of rice, dal and vegetables
mālāikāri মালাইকারি
a dish of prawns and dessicated coconut

Staples

Rice is the main staple dish and it is served with almost every meal in various forms. Normally, breakfast and evening snacks comprise bubbled or flaked rice with milk and a fruit or some condiment like *bhājā* or fried vegetables or egg. Bread, or *ruṭi,* is also consumed in great quantities.

muṛi	bubbled rice	মুড়ি
ciṛā	flaked rice	চিড়া
khoi	popcorn	খই
bhājā	fried	ভাজা
ḍāl	lentil	ডাল
p̃āuruṭi	bread (loaf)	পাঁউরুটি
ruṭi	bread (homemade)	রুটি

FOOD

Meat

Goat and sheep meat is the most common as Muslims do not eat pork and Hindus do not eat beef.

beef	*gōmāngso*	গোমাংস
fat	*corbi*	চর্বি
goat	*p̃āṭhā*	পাঁঠা
ham/pork	*suyōrer mangso*	শুয়োরের মাংস
lamb	*bhaṛā*	ভেড়া
liver	*meṭe*	মেটে
meat	*māngso*	মাংস
mutton	*bhāṛār māngso*	ভেড়ার মাংস
turtle	*kocchop*	কচ্ছপ

Poultry

bird	*pākhi*	পাখী
chicken	*murgii*	মুরগী
duck	*h̃ās*	হাঁস

Seafood

fish	*māch*	মাছ
prawn	*cingṛi māch*	চিংড়ি মাছ

Vegetables

beans	*borbōṭi*	বরবটি
cabbage	*b̃ādhākōpi*	বাঁধাকপি
carrot	*gājor*	গাজর
cauliflower	*fulkōpi*	ফুলকপি
eggplant	*begun*	বে গুন
green vegetables	*shāk*	শাক
mushroom	*chātu*	ছাতু
onion	*p̃eāj*	পেঁয়াজ
peas	*moṭor shuṭi*	মটরশুটি
potato	*ālu*	আলু
pumpkin	*kumṛō*	কুমড়ো

Fruit

banana	*kolā*	কলা
coconut	*nārkel*	নারকেল
dates	*khejur*	খেজুর
fig	*ḍumur*	ডুমুর
fruit	*fol*	ফল

grapes	*āngur*	আঙ্গুর
green coconut	*ḍāb*	ডাব
guava	*peyārā*	পেয়ারা
lemon	*lebu*	লেবু
mango	*ām*	আম
melon	*fuṭi*	ফুটি
orange	*komlā*	কমলা
papaya	*p̃epe*	পেঁপে
pineapple	*ānāros*	আনারস
plum	*kul*	কুল
watermelon	*tormuj*	তরমুজ

Dairy Products

butter	*mākhon*	মাখন
cheese	*ciij/poniir*	চীজ / পনীর
cream	*noni/sor*	ননী / সর
milk	*dudh*	দুধ
yoghurt	*doyi*	দই

Condiments

chilli	*lonkā*	লঙ্কা
cinnamon	*dārcini*	দারচিনি
cloves	*lobongo*	লবঙ্গ
garlic	*rosun*	রসুন
ginger	*ādā*	আদা
mustard	*sorshe*	সরষে
salt	*nun*	নুন
sugar	*cini*	চিনি
tumeric	*holud*	হলুদ
cumin	*jirā*	জিরা

Drinks

Alcoholic drinks (known as *mod*) are not served for social occasions. *Sorboṭ*, which is made from water, sugar and lemon, is often served as a drink. You will usually be offered a variety of fruit juices or extracts.

alcoholic drink/wine	*mod*	মদ
green coconut drink	*ḍāber jol*	ডাব

melon water	*tormuj*	তরমুজ
milk	*dudh*	দুধ
sorbet	*sorbot*	সরবত
tea	*cā*	চা
water	*jol/pāni* (B)	জল / পানি
boiled water	*fōṭānō jol*	ফোটানো জল
yoghurt drink	*lossi*	লস্যি

Shopping

Be prepared to negotiate your way around cramped and crowded shops. Bengalis are used to this and you will soon get used to it as well. You'll find plenty of shops on the main streets of cities and there are many markets where you can buy fresh produce daily. These markets have a great atmosphere and shopping there can be a very enjoyable and colourful experience. There are a great number of souvenirs to buy in Bengal so get ready to load your bags with reminders of your trip. If books are your passion, then Calcutta will satisfy any literary cravings with its many bookshops.

Where can I buy ...?
... kothāy pābo bolun to? ... কোথায় পাব বলুন ত?

Where is the nearest ...?	*kāchākāchi kothāy ... dōkān āche?*	কাছাকাছি কোথায় ... দোকান আছে?
bookshop	*bōier*	বইয়ের
chemist/pharmacy	*ōsudher*	ফুলের
florist	*fuler*	ভূষিমালের
grocery	*bhusimāler*	ওষুধের
shoe shop	*jutōr*	জুতোর
tailor	*dorjir*	দরজির
greengrocer	*sobjir*	সবজির

Service

Excuse me, Sir/Miss.
sunchen dādạ/didi — শুনছেন দাদা / দিদি

Can you help me?
āmāke aktu sāhājyo korben ki? — আমাকে একটু সাহায্য করবেন কি?

Sir/Miss I have been waiting for a long time.
ō dādā/didi āmi onekkhon opekkhā korchi — ও দাদা / দিদি, আমি অনেকক্ষণ অপেক্ষা করছি

I'd like to buy ...
āmi ... kinte cāi — আমি ... কিনতে চাই

How much is it?
eṭār koto dām? — এটার দাম কত?

Do you have another one?
ār āche? — আর আছে?

Can I see it?
ekṭu dekhte pāri? — একটু দেখতে পারি ?

bigger	*boṛo*	বড়
smaller	*chōṭo*	ছোট
cheaper	*sōsta*	সস্তা
more	*ārō*	আরো
less	*kom*	কম

Bargaining

There are only a few government-run stores which have fixed prices and there is no point bargaining there. But everywhere else, especially at markets, bargaining is expected.

It's expensive.
khub beshi dām cāichen খুব বেশী দাম চাইছেন
(lit: asking much)

I don't have much money.
āmār kāche beshi ṭākā neyi আমার কাছে বেশী টাকা নেই

You have to bring the price down.
dām ektu komāte hobe দাম একটু কমাতে হবে

Can you give me a discount?
kichu subidhā korte pāren ki? কিছু সুবিধা করতে পারেন কি?

I will give you ... rupees for it.
āmi er jonyo ... ṭākā debo আমি এর জন্য ... টাকা দেব

Clothing

clothing	*jāmākāpoṛ*	জামাকাপড়
coat/jacket	*kōṭ*	কোট
dress	*pōsāk*	পোষাক
hat	*ṭupi*	টুপি
jumper/sweater	*sōeṭār*	সোয়েটার

sandal	*cōṭi*	চটি
shirt	*jāmā*	জামা
shoe	*jutā*	জুতা
socks/stockings	*mōjā*	মোজা
trousers	*pant/pāthlun*	প্যান্ট / পাথলুন
underwear	*jāngiā/genji*	জাঙ্গিয়া / গেঞ্জী

Souvenirs

arts & crafts	*shilpo kāj*	শিল্পকাজ
embroidery	*sucishilpo*	শূচীশিল্প
pith ornaments	*shōlār goynā*	সোলার গয়না
conch shell ornaments	*s̃ākher goynā*	শাঁখের গয়না
batique	*bāṭik*	বাটিক্
mats	*matranchi*	মতরঞ্চি
saris	*shari*	শাড়ি

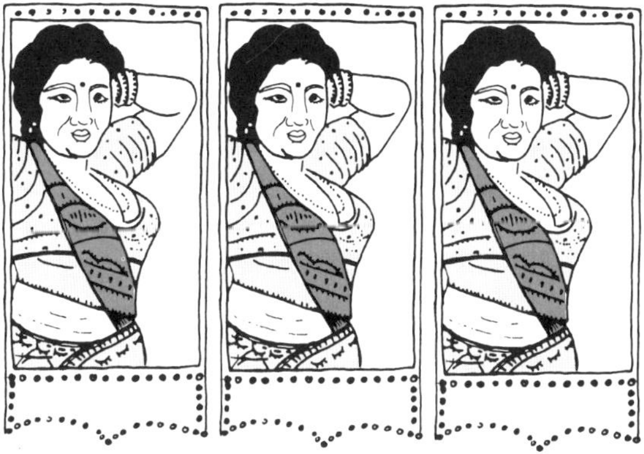

Toiletries

comb	*cirunii*	চিরুনি
condoms	*nirōdh*	নিরোধ
oil	*tel*	তেল
mirror	*āyonā*	আয়না
razor blades	*kshur/dāṛi kāṭār bleḍ*	ক্ষুর / দাড়ি কাটার ব্লেড
shampoo	*sāmpu*	স্যাম্পু
soap	*sābān*	সাবান
sunblock cream	*sunblok kriim*	সানব্লক ক্রীম
tampons	*tāmpons*	টেম্পনস্
tissues	*tisuz*	টিস্যুজ
toilet paper	*tōilet paypār*	টয়লেট পেপার
toothbrush	*tuthbrus*	টুথব্রাশ
toothpaste	*d̃āter mājon*	দাঁতের মাজন

Stationery & Publications

book	*bōi*	বই
dictionary	*ōvidhān*	অভিধান
envelope	*khām*	খাম
glue	*ā̃ṭhā*	আঁঠা
magazine	*sāmoik potrikā*	সাময়িক পত্রিকা
newspaper	*potrikā*	পত্রিকা
novel	*uponyās*	উপন্যাস
paper	*kāgoj*	কাগজ
pen	*kolom*	কলম
scissors	*k̃āci*	কাঁচি

Do you have any books/ newspapers in English?
ingrājite lekhā boi/ khoborer kāgoj āche ki?
ইংরাজিতে লেখা বই / খবরের কাগজ আছে কি?

Do you have a city map?
āpnār kāche sohorer māncitro āche? আপনার কাছে সহরের মানচিত্র আছে?

Photography

I'd like ... for this camera.	*ei kamerār jonno āmi ... cāi*	এই ক্যামেরার জন্য ... চাই
a battery	*batāri*	ব্যাটারী
B&W film	*film*	ফিল্ম
colour film	*rongin film*	রঙিন ফিল্ম
slide film	*transpārent film*	ট্রান্সপারেন্ট ফিল্ম

Can you please develop this?
ei filmṭā dhute pārben? এই ফিল্মটা ধুতে পারবেন?

When will it be ready?
kokhon tōiri hobe? কখন তৈরী হবে?

Smoking

cigarettes	*sigāret*	সিগারেট
matches	*diāsālāyi*	দিয়াশেলাই

May I smoke?
dhum pān korte pāri? ধুমপান করতে পারি?

Please don't smoke.
dhumpan korben nā ধুমপান করবেন ন না

Colours

black	*kālō*	কালো
blue	*niil*	নীল
brown	*bādāmii*	বাদামী
gold	*sōnāli*	সোনালী

green	*sobuj*	সবুজ
grey	*chāi*	ছাই
orange	*komla*	কমলা
pink	*pink*	পিঙ্ক
purple	*begunii*	বেগুনী
red	*lāl*	লাল
silver	*rupāli*	রুপালী
white	*sādā*	সাদা
yellow	*holud*	হলুদ
light	*hālkā*	হালকা
dark	*gaṛho*	গাঢ়

Some Useful Words

all	*sob/somosto*	সব / সমস্ত
every	*prottek*	প্রত্যেক
enough	*jothesṭo*	যথেষ্ট
many/much	*onek/prōcur*	অনেক / প্রচুর
little/few/a bit	*olpo/ekṭu/kichu*	অল্প / একটু / কিছু

Health

There is no health benefits system in Bengal. If you need medical assistance there are a number of alternatives; namely the traditional Indian system of medicine (*ayurvedic*), the homeopathic system of medicine (*unani*), the Graeco-Islamic system of medicine and Western medicine. Most hospitals and some private clinics practise Western medicine.

It is best not to drink water unless it is boiled and filtered, or to eat food from street vendors. Also it is unwise to walk barefoot or sleep without a mosquito net.

Where is the nearest ...?	*kāchākāchi ... kōthāyo bolun to?*	কাছাকাছি কোথায় ...বলুন ত?
doctor	*cikitsok/dāktār*	চিকিৎসক / ডাক্তার
chemist/pharmacy	*ōsudher dokān*	ওষুধের দোকান
hospital	*hāspātāl*	হাসপাতাল
dentist	*denṭisṭ*	ডেন্টিস্ট

Parts of the Body

ankle	*gōṛāli*	গোড়ালি
back	*piiṭh*	পীঠ
backbone	*siirdā̃ṛā*	শিরদাঁড়া
body	*shoriir*	শরীর
bone	*hāṛ*	হাড়

86 Parts of the Body

breast/chest	*buk/chāti*	বুক / ছাতি
buttock/hip	*pāchā*	পাছা
chin	*thutni*	থুৎনী
ear	*kān*	কান
fingers/toes	*āngul*	আঙ্গুল
heart	*hridoy*	হৃদয়
lips	*ṭ̃hōṭ*	ঠোঁট
mouth	*mukh*	মুখ
nail	*nokh*	নখ
neck/throat	*golā*	গলা
nose	*nāk*	নাক
skin	*cāmṛā*	চামড়া
thigh	*uru*	উরু
tooth	*d̃āt*	দাঁত
tongue	*jiv*	জিভ
wrist	*kōbji*	কবজি

Complaints

I feel dizzy. *āmār māthā ghurche*	আমার মাথা ঘুরছে
I feel weak. *āmār durbol lāgche*	আমার দুর্ব্বল লাগছে
She/He is ill. *ōr osukh*	ওর অসুখ
I've been bitten. *āmāke kise kāmṛeche*	আমাকে কিসে কামড়েছে
I have a headache. *āmār māthā dhoreche*	আমার মাথা ধরেছে
I have a sore throat/toothache. *āmār golā/d̃āt byāthā kōrche*	আমার গলা / দাঁত ব্যাথা করছে
I have a rash. *āmār gāye ki sob beriyeche*	আমার গায়ে কি সব বেরিয়েছে
I burned my ... *āmār ... puṛe giyeche*	আমার ... পুড়ে গিয়েছে

I have ...	*āmār .. hōyeche*	আমার ... হয়েছে
constipation	*kosṭhokāṭhinnyo*	কোষ্ঠকাঠিন্য
a cold/flu	*sordi*	সর্দ্দি
a cough	*kāshi*	কাশি
diarrhoea/ dysentry	*ōlāuṭhā*	ওলাউঠা
a fever	*jwor*	জ্বর
food poisoning	*peṭ khārāp*	পেট খারাপ
an itch	*culkāni*	চুলকানি

Women's Health

I want to see a ...	*āmi ... dekhāte cai*	আমি ... দেখাতে চাই
female doctor	*mohilā cikitsok*	মহিলা চিকিৎসক
gynaecologist	*strii cikitsok*	স্ত্রী চিকিৎসক

I haven't menstruated for ... months.
āmār ... mās māsik hoyni — আমার ... মাস মাসিক হয়নি

I'm pregnant.
āmi ontoswottā/gorvobotii — আমি অন্তস্বত্ত্বা / গর্ভবতী

I'm on the pill.
āmi pil khāi — আমি পিল খাই

At the Chemist

I need something for ...
āmāke ...r jonnyo kichu din — আমাকে ...র জন্য কিছু দিন

I have a prescription.
āmār kāche preskripsān āche — আমার কাছে প্রেসক্রিপশন আছে

How many times a day?
dine koto bār? — দিনে কত বার ?

Band-aids	*poṭṭi*	পট্টি
aspirin	*aspirin*	এ্যাস্‌পিরিন
condoms	*nirōdh*	নিরোধ
cough mixture	*kāsir ōsudh*	কাশির ওষুধ
eyedrops	*cōkher ōsudh*	চোখের ওষুধ
insect repellent	*pōkamākōrer ōsudh*	পোকামাকড়ের ওষুধ
laxatives	*pāikhānār ōsudh*	পায়খানার ওষুধ
painkillers	*byatha komānōr ōsudh*	ব্যাথা কমাবার ওষুধ

Some Useful Words & Phrases

I'm feeling better now.
āmi ekhon vālo bōdh kōrchi — আমি এখন ভাল বোধ করছি

I have my own syringe.
āmār kāche sirinj āche — আমার কাছে সিরিন্জ আছে

I'm allergic to ...	*āmār ...-e alārgi*	আমার ... এ এলার্জি
antibiotics	*anṭi bāioṭik*	এ্যান্টিবায়োটিক
aspirin	*aspirin*	এ্যাস্পিরিন
penicillin	*penisilin*	পেনিসিলিন

I'm ...	*āmār ... āche*	আমার ... আছে
asthmatic	*sāsh kosṭo*	শ্বাস কষ্ট
diabetic	*bōhumutro*	বহু মূত্র
epileptic	*mrigii/sonnyāsh rōg*	মৃগী / সন্ন্যাস রোগ

accident	*durghoṭonā*	দুর্ঘটনা
addiction	*neshā*	নেশা
AIDS	*AIDS*	এইড্স্
anaemia	*roktohiinotā*	রক্তহীনতা
contraceptive	*jonmo niyontron*	জন্মনিয়ন্ত্রণ
blood	*rokto/khun* (B)	রক্ত / খুন
blood pressure	*roktocāp*	রক্তচাপ
burn	*pōṛā*	পোড়া
contagious	*c͠hōāce*	ছোঁয়াচে
cramps	*khil dhorā*	খিল ধরা
delirious	*bhul bokā*	ভুল বকা
disease	*rōg*	রোগ
hepatitis	*hepāṭiṭis*	হেপাটাইটিস্
injection	*injekson*	ইনজেক্শান্

insomnia	*onidrā*	অনিদ্রা
medicine	*ōsudh*	ওষুধ
pain/ache	*byathā*	ব্যাথা
poison	*bish*	বিষ
sunstroke	*rōdh lāgā*	রোদ লাগা
swollen	*phuleche*	ফুলেছে
urine	*pecchāp*	পেচ্ছাপ
vitamins	*viṭamin*	ভিটামিন
vomit	*bomi*	বমি

Time, Dates & Festivals

To differentiate between am and pm, use the words *sokāl* ('morning'), *bikel* ('afternoon'), *sōndhyā* ('evening') and *rāt* (night).

Telling the Time

What time is it? *koṭā bāje/akhon somoi koto?*	কটা বাজে / এখন সময় কত ?

It is ... now.	*akhon ...*	এখন ...
7 am	*sokāl sāttā*	সকাল সাতটা
4 pm	*bikel cārṭā*	বিকেল চারটা
6 pm	*sōndhyā choṭa*	সন্ধ্যা ছটা
10 pm	*rāt doshṭā*	রাত দশটা

Use the word *pōune* to indicate 'a quarter to'. 'A quarter past' is *sōyā* and 'half past' is *sāṛe.*

3.15 pm	*bikel sōyā tinṭe*	বিকেল সোয়া তিনটে
7.30 am	*sokāl sāre sāttā*	সকাল সাড়ে সাতটা
5.45 pm	*sōndhyā pōune choṭā*	সন্ধ্যা পৌনে ছটা

During the Day

dawn	*bhōr*	ভোর
morning	*sokāl*	সকাল
noon	*dupur*	দুপুর
afternoon	*bikel*	বিকেল
dusk	*gōdhuli*	গোধুলি
evening	*sondhyā*	সন্ধ্যা
night	*rāt*	রাত
midnight	*dupur rāt*	দুপুর রাত

Present

now/immediately	*akhoni*	এখনি
today	*āj*	আজ
this ...	*āj/eyi ...*	আজ ... / এই ...
morning	*sokāl*	সকাল
afternoon	*bikel*	বিকেল

(NB *eyi* is only used when 'at this particular time' is stressed.)

Past

yesterday	*(goto) kāl*	(গত) কাল
day before yesterday	*(goto) porshu*	(গত) পরশু
last ...	*goto ...*	গত ...
night	*rāt*	রাত
week	*soptāho*	সপ্তাহ
month	*mās*	মাস
year	*bochor*	বছর
yesterday ...	*gotokāl ...*	গতকাল ...
morning	*sokāl*	সকাল
afternoon	*bikel*	বিকেল
evening	*sondhyā*	সন্ধ্যা

Future

tomorrow	*(āgāmi) kāl*	(আগামী) কাল
tomorrow ...	*āgāmi kāl ...*	আগামী কাল ...
morning	*sokāl*	সকাল
afternoon	*bikel*	বিকেল
evening	*sondhyā*	সন্ধ্যা রাত
night	*rāt*	রাত
next ...	*āgāmi ...*	আগামী ...
week	*soptāho*	সপ্তাহ
month	*mās*	মাস
year	*bochor*	বছর

Days of the Week

What day is it today?
āj ki bār? আজ কি বার?

It's ... *āj ...* আজ ...

Monday *sōmbār* সোমবার	Tuesday *mongolbār* মঙ্গলবার	Wednesday *budhbār* বুধবার	Thursday *brihospotibār* বৃহস্পতি বার
Friday *sukrobār* শুক্রবার	Saturday *shonibār* শনিবার	Sunday *robibār* রবিবার	

Bengali Calendar & Seasons

The Bengali calendar is 593-594 years behind the Gregorian calendar; 1996 AD is then 1402 Bengali year. A year has 365 days – 12 months of 29-32 days. There are six seasons in a year. Each season lasts for two months.

Seasons

summer	*griishmo*	গ্রীষ্ম
rainy	*borshā*	বর্ষা
autumn	*shorot*	শরৎ
harvesting	*hemonto*	হেমন্ত
winter	*shiit*	শীত
spring	*bosonto*	বসন্ত

Months

The first Bengali month is around mid-April on the English calender.

bōisāk	(mid-April – mid-May)	বৈশাখ
jōishṭho	(mid-May – mid-June)	জ্যৈষ্ঠ
āshāṛ	(mid-June – mid-July)	আষাঢ়
shrābon	(mid-July – mid-August)	শ্রাবণ
bhādro	(mid-Aug – mid-Sep)	ভাদ্র
āshwin	(mid-Sep – mid-Oct)	আশ্বিন
kārtik	(mid-Oct – mid-Nov)	কার্তিক
ogrohāyon	(mid-Nov – mid-Dec)	অগ্রহায়ণ
pōus	(mid-Dec – mid-Jan)	পৌষ
māgh	(mid-Jan – mid-Feb)	মাঘ
fālgun	(mid-Feb – mid-March)	ফাল্গুন
cōitro	(mid-March – mid-April)	চৈত্র

Some Useful Words

after	*pore*	পরে
all day	*sārādin*	সারাদিন
always	*sob somoy/sorbodā*	সবসময় / সর্ব্বদা
annual	*bārshikii*	বার্ষিকী
anytime/whenever	*jokhon*	যখন
before	*āge*	আগে
century	*shotābdi*	শতাব্দী
day	*din*	দিন
decade	*dosok*	দশক
early/quick/soon	*shiggiir/tāṛātāṛi*	শিগগীর / তাড়াতাড়ি
era	*kāl/jug*	কাল / যুগ
everyday	*sob din*	সবদিন
forever	*cirokāl*	চিরকাল
fortnight	*pokkhokāl*	পক্ষকাল
holiday	*chuṭi*	ছুটি
hour	*ghonṭā*	ঘন্টা
late	*derii*	দেরী
month	*mās*	মাস
never	*kokhonō-nā*	কখনো না
nowadays	*ājkāl*	আজকাল
recently	*idāning*	ইদানিং
sometimes	*kokhonō*	কখনো
then	*tokhon*	তখন
time	*somoyo*	সময়
week	*soptāho/hoptā*	সপ্তাহ / হপ্তা
a while ago	*kichu din āge*	কিছুদিন আগে
year	*bochor*	বছর
span of 12 years	*jug*	যুগ

Festivals

With the exception of Bengali New Year all festivals are religious. While Muslims celebrate *Eid-ul-Fitr* and *Eid-ul-Azha*, Christians celebrate their own festivals. For Hindus there are many festivals because there are many gods. Most festivals however are celebrated by everyone, irrespective of religion.

Poylā boisāk (April-May)
The beginning of the Bengali New Year. Traditionally, this was when all official book-keeping began and was called *Halkhata*. It is now celebrated by ushering in the new year.

Muslim Festivals

Eid-ul Fitr (April-May)
Fasting for one month to appreciate the plight of the poor who go hungry. This is usually followed by a celebration.

Eid-ul-Azha (2 months & 10 days after *Eid-ul-Fitr*)
Traditionally this is the day of sacrificing what is dearest to

you. These days a cow or goat is sacrificed and the meat is shared amongst relatives and those who cannot afford meat.

Muharram (3rd week of June)
The first month of the Arabic calendar year. Muslims commemorate a religious war which occurred in the desert (called the Karbala War) when Imam Hasan and Iman Husain, grandsons of the prophet Hazrat Muhammed, sacrificed their lives for their religion. Hundreds of people died in the desert without water. Muslims celebrate this war by mourning, fasting and praying.

Hindu Festivals

Hindus have many gods, and festivities continue throughout the year. Some of these are celebrated by Bengalis of all religions and are recognised by the government as public holidays.

Swaraswati Puja (mid-Feb)
Worship of Swaraswati, goddess of learning and the daughter of Siva and Durga. Young children are introduced to books and learning during this festival.

Holi/Dol-jatra (3rd week of March)
Festival of colours in honour of Krishna, an incarnation of the god Vishnu and an important figure in the epic poem *Mahabharata*.

Durga Puja (Sept-Oct)
Largest festival in Bengal, celebrating the slaying of the demon by the goddess Durga and, thus, the restoration of peace. It is a time of family reunion. At the end of four days

of celebration, everyone exchanges good wishes with each other and reconciles with enemies.

Rakhi/Bhai (Oct-Nov)
Festival of brotherhood, when people tie a thread of friendship around others' wrists. Sisters entertain brothers to a feast.

Dipavali (Oct-Nov)
Festival of lights, dedicated to Lakshmi, goddess of wealth and daughter of Durga.

Gods & Prominent Beings

Ganesh
Elephant-headed son of Durga and god of wisdom. No offering to any god is done before worshipping Ganesh. His vehicle is a shrew.

Brahma

First member of the Hindu Trinity – creator of all worldly beings. His consort is Swaraswati and his vehicle a swan.

Durga

Destructive form of Parvati, Siva's consort. Carried by a lion, she kills the demon Mohishasur to bring peace.

Indra

King of gods and the God of rain. His vehicle is an elephant called Oirabat.

Kali/Sakti

Destructive form of Parvati. She wears a garland of human heads in order to frighten the world. She is stopped only by her consort Siva, who she steps on by mistake and comes to her senses.

Kartik

Handsome son of Durga, commander of Indra's army. His vehicle is a peacock. He is looked upon as the handsome, ideal groom.

Lakshmi

Wife of Vishnu and goddess of wealth and prosperity. Her vehicle is an owl.

Madan

God of love. His consort is Rati, a synonym for love-making. He casts an arrow of flowers to induce the feeling of love in all human beings.

Swaraswati

Daughter of Durga and Goddess of learning and music. Her consort is Brahma. Her vehicle is a swan.

Krishna

An incarnation of Vishnu, hero of *Mahabharata* and originator of the holy Gita. He is also a fun-loving, promiscuous cowherd, longed for by many cowherdesses. Though he has a wife, he is well-known for his affairs with his maternal aunt, Radha.

Narayan/Vishnu

Second member of the Hindu Trinity; the Preserver. His consort is Lakshmi. Narada is his constant companion and disciple, and his vehicle is Garuda, a bird.

Rama

An incarnation of Vishnu and the hero of the epic *Ramayana*. His wife is Sita and his devoted brother is Lakshmana. Hanuman, a monkey, is his devoted disciple.

Shiva

Third member of the Hindu Trinity; the Destroyer. His consort is Parvati. Both symbolise the union of male and female and are represented as idols in Hindu temples. His vehicle is a bull called Nandi. He has various forms including Pashupati, Mahadev and Nataraj, the God of dancing.

Some Useful Words

āroti — আরতি
worship with lamp

āhuti/onjoli — আহুতি / অঞ্জলি
sacrifice

bhōg — ভোগ
food for offering to gods

bisorjon — বিসর্জন
a farewell to a god

dikshā/montro — দিক্ষা / মন্ত্র
seeds of wisdom bestowed upon the disciple by the guru

coronāmrito — চরণামৃত
holy water

dhuup — ধূপ
joss sticks

dhyan — ধ্যান
meditation

grontho — গ্রন্থ
the holy book

guru — গুরু
the preacher

jogābhyās — যোগাভ্যাস
the practice of yoga

kormo — কর্ম
laws of cause and effect

melā — মেলা
fair

Mohābhārot — মহাভারত
literary epic about the battle between two families and the god, Krishna

mondop — মণ্ডপ
pavilion

mondir — মন্দির
temple

montro — মন্ত্র
prayer; magic spell

mānot/sopoth/sonkolpo — মানত / শপথ / সংকল্প
vow

mōksho/nirbān — মোক্ষ / নির্বাণ
emancipation

omābosyā — অমাবস্যা
the dark moon

pāp — পাপ
vice/sin

prasād — প্রসাদ
food that has been offered previously to a god

prārthonā — প্রার্থনা
prayer

pujā — পূজা
worship

punyo — পুণ্য
a good deed

purnimā — পূর্ণিমা
a full moon

Rāmāyon — রামায়ন
Hindu epic about Rama and Sita

roth রথ
chariot/vehicle of a god

sādhu সাধু
an ascetic

shishyo শিষ্য
disciple

somādhi সমাধি
deep meditation

songsār সংসার
family/worldly life

ṭikā টীকা
auspicious mark on the forehead

jogii যোগী
holy man

Numbers & Amounts

Numbers in Bengali follow a similar pattern to numbers in English. For instance, thirty-five (*p̃oytrish*), uses the words for thirty (*trish*) and five (*p̃āc*). Bengali numbers, however, are complicated in that they change slightly or are shortened when used in conjunction with another number. So, unless you memorise the words for all numbers, you will have difficulty forming them. If you want to say a number such as seventy-eight (*āṭāttōr*), use the words for eight (*āṭ*) and seventy (*sōttōr*). You will not be absolutely correct but you will get the message across.

Cardinal Numbers

1	*ak*	এক
2	*dui*	দুই
3	*tin*	তিন
4	*cār*	চার
5	*p̃āc*	পাঁচ
6	*choy*	ছয়
7	*sāt*	সাত
8	*āṭ*	আট
9	*noy*	নয়
10	*dosh*	দশ
11	*agārō*	এগারো
12	*bārō*	বারো

13	*tarō*	তেরো
14	*cōddō*	চোদ্দ
15	*ponerō*	পনেরো
16	*shōlō*	ষোল
17	*soterō*	সতেরো
18	*āṭhārō*	আঠারো
19	*unish*	উনিশ
20	*kuṛi/bish*	কুড়ি / বিশ
30	*tirish/trish*	তিরিশ / ত্রিশ
40	*collish*	চল্লিশ
50	*poncāsh*	পঞ্চাশ
60	*shāṭ*	ষাট
70	*sōttōr*	সত্তর
80	*āshii*	আশি
90	*nobbōyi*	নব্বই
100	*akso\sho*	একশ / শ
1000	*hājār*	হাজার
1,000,000	*lākh/lokkho*	লাখ / লক্ষ
10,000,000	*kōṭi*	কোটি

Ordinal Numbers

1st	*prothom*	প্রথম
2nd	*dwitiyo*	দ্বিতীয়
3rd	*tritiyo*	তৃতীয়
4th	*coturtho*	চতুর্থ
5th	*poncom*	পঞ্চম
6th	*shoshṭho*	ষষ্ঠ
7th	*soptom*	সপ্তম
8th	*oshṭom*	অষ্টম
9th	*nobom*	নবম
10th	*doshom*	দশম

Days of the Month

1st	*poylā*	পয়লা
2nd	*dōsorā*	দোসরা
3rd	*tesorā*	তেসরা
4th	*cōuṭhā*	চৌঠা
5th	*pācoyi*	পাঁচই
6th	*choyi*	ছই
7th	*sātoyi*	সাতই
8th	*āṭoyi*	আটই
9th	*noyi*	নই
10th	*doshoyi*	দশই
11th	*egāroyi*	এগারই
12th	*bāroyi*	বারই
13th	*teroyi*	তেরই
14th	*cōddoyi*	চৌদ্দই
15th	*poneroyi*	পনরই
16th	*shōloyi*	ষোলই
17th	*soteroyi*	সতেরই
18th	*āṭhāroyi*	আঠারই
19th	*unishe*	উনিশে
20th	*bishe*	বিশে
21st	*ekushe*	একুশে
22nd	*bāishe*	বাইশে
23rd	*teyishe*	তেইশে
24th	*cobbishe*	চব্বিশে
25th	*pocishe*	পঁচিশে
26th	*chābbishe*	ছাব্বিশে
27th	*sātāshe*	সাতাশে
28th	*āṭhāshe*	আটাশে
29th	*untrishe*	উনত্রিশে
30th	*trishe*	ত্রিশে

31st	*ektrishe*	একত্রিশে
32nd	*bottrishe*	বত্রিশে

Fractions

¼	*siki*	সিকি
½	*ādhā*	আধা
1½	*deṛ*	দেড়
2½	*āṛāi*	আড়াই

Some Useful Words

count	*gōnā*	গোনা
enough	*jotheshṭo*	যথেষ্ট
equal	*somān*	সমান
few	*kichu*	কিছু
how much/many?	*koto?*	কত
little (amount)	*olpo*	অল্প
many	*onek*	অনেক
maximum	*boṛojōr*	বড়জোর
minimum/at least	*ontoto*	অন্ততঃ
numerous	*osongkho*	অসংখ্য
once	*akbār*	একবার
pair	*jōṛā*	জোড়া
size	*māp*	মাপ
too much	*procur*	প্রচুর
12 years	*jug*	যুগ
weight	*ōjon*	ওজন

Vocabulary

A

a/an/one	*ak/akṭā/ekṭi*	এক / একটি / একটা
able, to be	*sokkhom*	সক্ষম
I can do it.	*āmi pāri*	আমি পারি
Can you do it?	*tumi pārbe ki?*	তুমি পারবে কি?
abortion	*gorvopāt*	গর্ভপাত
about	*sombondhe*	সম্বন্ধে
above	*upore*	উপরে
abroad	*bidesh*	বিদেশ
accept	*mene neōā*	মেনে নেওয়া
I accept.	*āmi mānchi*	আমি মানছি
accident	*durghoṭonā*	দুর্ঘটনা
accommodation	*bāsā/thākār jāygā*	বাসা / থাকার জায়গা
ache	*bathā*	ব্যাথা
across	*ōpāre*	ওপারে
adaptor	*aḍāpṭār*	এ্যাডাপ্‌টার
addict	*neshākhōr*	নেশাখোর
addiction	*neshā*	নেশা
address	*ṭhikānā*	ঠিকানা
administration	*shāshon/sorkār*	শাসন / সরকার
admire	*proshongshā*	প্রশংসা
admit (allow in)	*probesh korā/ḍhōkā*	প্রবেশ করা / ঢোকা
admit (confess)	*swikar kōrā*	স্বীকার করা
adventure	*obhijān*	অভিযান
advice	*upodes/jukti*	উপদেশ / যুক্তি
advise	*upodes deyoā*	উপদেশ দেওয়া
aeroplane	*uṛōjāhāj*	উড়োজাহাজ

afraid	*bhiito*	ভীত
after	*pore*	পরে
afternoon	*bikel/bikāl*	বিকেল / বিকাল
again	*ābār*	আবার
against	*biruddhe*	বিরুদ্ধে
age	*boyos*	বয়স
agree	*rāji*	রাজী
I agree.	*āmi rāji*	আমি রাজী
Do you agree?	*tumi rāji ki?*	তুমি রাজী কি?
agriculture	*krishi*	কৃষি
air	*bātās/hāōyā*	বাতাস / হাওয়া
air-conditioned	*sita-tāp niyontrito*	শীততাপ নিয়ন্ত্রিত
airline	*bimān*	বিমান
airmail	*hāōāi ciṭhi*	হাওয়াই চিঠি
alarm clock	*ghoṛi*	ঘড়ি
airport	*bimān bondor*	বিমান বন্দর
alcohol	*mod*	মদ
alive	*jiibito*	জীবিত
all	*sob/sokol/somosto*	সব / সকল / সমস্ত
Alright/OK.	*ācchā/ṭhik*	আচ্ছা / ঠিক
almost	*prāyo*	প্রায়
alone	*akā*	একা
along	*borābor*	বরাবর
also/and	*ebong/ō/ār*	এবং / ও / আর
alter	*bodlānō*	বদলানো
alternative	*bikolpo*	বিকল্প
although	*jōdiyō*	যদিও
always	*sob somoyo/ sorbodā*	সবসময় / সর্ব্বদা
ambassador	*rāstrodut*	রাষ্ট্রদূত
among	*moddhe*	মধ্যে

ancient	*prāciin*	প্রাচীন
and/also	*ebong/ō/ār*	এবং / ও / আর
anger	*rāg*	রাগ
angry	*kruddho/rāgii*	ক্রুদ্ধ / রাগী
animal	*jōntu/poshu/janōār*	জন্তু / পশু / জানোয়ার
answer (n)	*jobāb/uttor*	জবাব / উত্তর
answer (v)	*(jobāb/uttor) deyoā*	জবাব / উত্তর দেওয়া
antique	*prācin*	প্রাচীন
any	*keu* (p)/*jekōnō* (int)	কেউ / যেকোন
appointment (job)	*cākri*	চাকরি
approximate	*kāchākāchi*	কাছাকাছি
argument	*torko*	তর্ক
arrive	*põuchānō*	পৌঁছানো
art	*shilpo*	শিল্প
ashtray	*chāi-dān*	ছাইদান
ask (n)	*proshno/jiggãsā*	প্রশ্ন / জিজ্ঞাসা
ask (v)	*(proshno/jiggãsā) korā*	প্রশ্ন / জিজ্ঞাসা করা
at	*-o/-e/-te*	-য় / -এ / -তে
automatic	*swoyongkriyo*	স্বয়ংক্রিয়
awaken (v)	*jāgō/uṭhō*	জাগো / উঠো

B

baby	*bāccā/shishu*	বাচ্চা / শিশু
backpack	*bōjhā*	বোঝা
bad	*khārāp/mondo*	খারাপ / মন্দ
bag	*tholi*	থলি
baggage	*māl*	মাল
ball	*bol*	বল
bank	*bank*	ব্যাঙ্ক
bar (place)	*s̃uṛikhānā*	শুঁড়িখানা

VOCABULARY

barber	*nāpit*	নাপিত
basic	*mul*	মূল
bath	*cān/snān*	চান / স্নান
battery	*bāṭāri*	ব্যাটারী
be (v)	*howā*	হওয়া
beautiful	*sundor/sushrii*	সুন্দর / সুশ্রী
because	*kāron/kanonā/jehetu*	কারণ / কেননা / যেহেতু
bed	*bichānā*	বিছানা
bedbugs	*chārpōkā*	ছারপোকা
before	*āge/sāmne*	আগে / সামনে
beggar	*vikhāri/vikkhuk*	ভিখারী / ভিক্ষুক
begin	*āromvo/suru*	আরম্ভ / শুরু
beginner	*chatro*	ছাত্র
behind	*pichone*	পিছনে
bell	*ghonṭā*	ঘন্টা
below	*niice*	নীচে
beside	*pāshe*	পাশে
best	*sobceye valō*	সবচেয়ে ভালো
better than ...	*...-r ceye valō*	... র চেয়ে ভালো
between	*moddhye*	মধ্যে
beyond	*dure/periye*	দুরে / পেরিয়ে
bicycle	*sāikel*	সাইকেল
big	*boṛo*	বড়
bird	*pākhii*	পাখী
birth	*jonmo*	জন্ম
birthday	*jonmōdin*	জন্মদিন
bitter	*tetō/titā*	তেতো / তিতা
blessing	*āshiirbād*	আশীর্ব্বাদ
blind	*ondho*	অন্ধ
boat	*nōukā*	নৌকা
body	*shōriir*	শরীর

VOCABULARY

boil (v)	*fōṭānō*	ফোটানো
bomb	*bōmā*	বোমা
book	*bōi*	বই
boring	*akgheye*	একঘেয়ে
I'm bored.	*āmār akgheye lāgche*	আমার একঘেয়ে লাগছে
borrow	*dhār*	ধার
May I borrow this?	*āmi eṭā dhār nite pāri?*	আমি এটা ধার নিতে পারি?
boss	*upor wālā* (Hindi)	উপরওয়ালা
both	*uvoye/dujone*	উভয়ে / দুজনে
bottle	*bōtol*	বোতল
bottle opener	*bōtol khōlār jāntro*	বোতল খোলার যন্ত্র
bow (v)	*niicu*	নীচু
bowl	*bāṭi*	বাটি
boy	*chele*	ছেলে
boyfriend	*chele bondhu*	ছেলে বন্ধু
brave	*sāhosi*	সাহসী
break (v)	*vāngā*	ভাঙ্গা
breakfast	*prātorāsh*	প্রাতরাশ
breath	*nisswās*	নিশ্বাস
breeze	*hāōwā/bātās*	হাওয়া / বাতাস
bribe (n)	*ghus*	ঘুষ
bribe, to give a	*ghus deōyā*	ঘুষ দেওয়া
bribe, to take a	*ghus neōyā*	ঘুষ নেওয়া
bridge	*pul/setu*	পুল. / সেতু
bright	*jhokmoke/jomkālō*	ঝকমকে / জমকালো
bring	*ānō*	আনো
Please bring the paper.	*kāgojṭā ānō*	কাগজটা আনো
broken	*bhāngā*	ভাঙ্গা

VOCABULARY

broom	*jhāṭā*	ঝাঁটা
brothel	*beshyābāṛi*	বেশ্যাবাড়ি
bucket	*bālti*	বালতি
bug	*pōkā*	পোকা
building	*bāṛi*	বাড়ি
burn (n)	*pōṛā*	পোড়া
burn (v)	*puṛe giyeche*	পুড়ে গিয়েছে
business	*babsā*	ব্যাবসা
busy	*basto*	ব্যস্ত
but	*kintu*	কিন্তু
buy (v)	*kenā*	কেনা
I'd like to buy ...	*āmi ... kinte cāi*	আমি ... কিনতে চাই

C

call (v)	*ḍākā*	ডাকা
camp	*tābu*	তাঁবু
Can we camp here?	*āmrā ekhāne tābu khāṭāte pāri?*	আমরা এখানে তাঁবু খাঁটাতে পারি?
can (v)	*pārā*	পারা
I can do this.	*āmi pāri*	আমি পারি
I can't do this.	*āmi pāri nā*	আমি পারি না
can (tin)	*ṭin*	টিন
can opener	*ṭin khōlār jāntro*	টিন খোলার যন্ত্র
cancel	*nākoc/bātil*	নাকচ / বাতিল
candle	*mōmbāti*	মোমবাতি
cap	*ṭupi*	টুপি
capital (of a city)	*rājdhāni*	রাজধানী
capital (money)	*muldhon*	মূলধন
capitalism	*pujibād*	পুঁজিবাদ
car	*gāṛi*	গাড়ি
cards (playing)	*tās*	তাস

VOCABULARY

care	*jotno*	যত্ন
Take care.	*jotno niyō*	যত্ন নিও
careful	*sābdhān*	সাবধান
cashier	*koshādkyoksho*	কোষাধ্যক্ষ
cave	*guhā*	গুহা
cemetery	*koborkhānā/ gōrosthān* (B)	কবরখানা / গোরস্থান (B)
centre, at the	*mājhkhāne*	মাঝখানে
century	*shotābdii*	শতাব্দী
certain	*niscit/niswongsoy*	নিশ্চিত / নিঃশংসয়
I am certain.	*āmi niscit*	আমি নিশ্চিত
Are you certain?	*āpni niscit ki?*	আপনি নিশ্চিত কি?
certainly	*niscoyo*	নিশ্চয়
chair	*ceār/kurshi* (B)	চেয়ার. / কুরশি
chance	*sujōg*	সুযোগ
change (coins)	*khucrō*	খুচরো
change (v)	*bodlāno*	বদলানো
cheap	*sostā*	সস্তা
chemist (pharmacy)	*ōsudher dōkān*	ওষুধের দোকান
child	*shishu/bāccā*	শিশু / বাচ্চা
choice	*pochondo*	পছন্দ
choose	*bāchā*	বাছা
Christmas	*boṛodin*	বড়দিন
church	*giirjā*	গির্জা
cigarettes	*sigāreṭ*	সিগারেট
city	*sohor/nogor*	সহর / নগর
clean (adj)	*poriskār*	পরিস্কার
close (v)	*ḍhākā*	ঢাকা
close (nearby)	*kāchā kāchi/āse pāshe*	কাছাকাছি / আশেপাশে
closed	*bondho*	বন্ধ

VOCABULARY

cloth	*kāpoṛ*	কাপড়
clothing	*jāmākāpoṛ*	জামাকাপড়
cloud	*megh*	মেঘ
cockroach	*ārsōlā*	আরসোলা
cold (temp)	*ṭhānḍā/shiit*	ঠান্ডা / শীত
colour	*rong*	রং
come	*āsā*	আসা
Can I/we come?	*āste pāri?*	আসতে পারি?
Are you coming?	*āschen ki?*	আসছেন কি?
comfort	*ārām*	আরাম
communism	*gonosāmyobādi*	গণসাম্যবাদী
complaint	*nāliish*	নালিশ
completely	*purō/sompurno*	পুরো / সম্পুর্ণ
complex	*joṭil*	জটিল
conceal (v)	*ḍhākā*	ঢাকা
condom	*nirodh* (lit: protection)	নিরোধ
Congratulations!	*obhinondon*	অভিনন্দন
consulate	*dutābās*	দূতাবাস
contact (v)	*c̃hōā*	ছোঁয়া
contraceptive	*jonmo-niyontron*	জন্মনিয়ন্ত্রণ
contract	*cukti*	চুক্তি
conversation	*kothābārtā*	কথাবার্ত্তা
cooperation	*sohojōgitā*	সহযোগীতা
copper	*tāmā*	তামা
coral	*probāl*	প্রবাল
cook (v)	*rānnā*	রান্না
cook (n)	*r̃ādhuni*	রাঁধুনী
corner	*kōnā*	কোনা
correct (n)	*ṭhik*	ঠিক
corrupt	*osot*	অসৎ

cost	*dām*	দাম
How much does it cost?	*er dām koto?*	এর দাম কি?
cot	*khāt/cōuki*	খাট / চৌকি
count (v)	*gōnā*	গোনা
country	*desh*	দেশ
countryside	*grām*	গ্রাম
court	*ādālot*	আদালত
crazy	*pāgol*	পাগল
cross (angry)	*rāg*	রাগ
crossroad	*cōumāthā*	চৌমাথা
customs duty	*sulko*	শুল্ক

D

daily	*protyoho/protidin*	প্রত্যহ / প্রতিদিন
damp	*s̃ats̃ete*	স্যাঁতসেঁতে
danger	*bipod*	বিপদ
dark	*ondhokār*	অন্ধকার
date (time)	*tārikh*	তারিখ
dawn	*bhōr/protyush*	ভোর / প্রত্যুষ
day	*din*	দিন
dead	*morā/mrito*	মরা / মৃত
deaf	*kālā*	কালা
death	*mrityu*	মৃত্যু
decide	*monosthir korā*	মন স্থির করা
decision	*siddhānto*	সিদ্ধান্ত
deep	*gōviir*	গভীর
delay	*derii/bilombo*	দেরী / বিলম্ব
delicious	*suswādu*	সুস্বাদু
delirious	*bhul bokā*	ভুল বকা
democracy	*gonotontro*	গণতন্ত্র

demonstration (protest)	*michil*	মিছিল
deny	*oswiikār*	অস্বীকার
departure	*prosthān*	প্রস্থান
deposit	*gocchit*	গচ্ছিত
desert	*morubhumi*	মরুভূমি
destroy	*dhwongso*	ধ্বংস
detail	*k̃huṭināṭi*	খুঁটিনাটি
development	*unnoyon*	উন্নয়ন
dictatorship	*ekonāyokotwo*	একনায়কত্ব
dictionary	*ōvidhān*	অভিধান
different	*vinno/onyo rokom*	ভিন্ন / অন্যরকম
difficult	*koṭhin/sokto*	কঠিন / শক্ত
dinner	*rāter khābār*	রাতের খাবার
direction	*dik*	দিক
dirty	*moyolā*	ময়লা
disadvantage	*osubidha*	অসুবিধা
discount	*bāṭā*	বাটা
discover	*ābiskār*	আবিস্কার
discrimination	*pokhyopātitwo*	পক্ষপাতিত্ব
distant	*dur*	দুর
disturb	*baghāt*	ব্যাঘাত
do	*korā*	করা
Will you do it?	*tumi korbe ki?*	তুমি করবে কি?
dock (n)	*pāṭāton*	পাটাতন
doctor	*cikitsok/dāktār*	চিকিৎসক / ডাক্তার
doll	*putul*	পুতুল
door	*dorojā*	দরজা
double	*dwigun/jugol*	দ্বিগুণ / যুগল
doubt	*sondeho*	সন্দেহ
down	*niice*	নীচে

VOCABULARY

drawing	*noksā*	নক্সা
dream	*swopno*	স্বপ্ন
drink (n)	*pāniiyo*	পানীয়
drink (v)	*khāōyā*	খাওয়া
drive (v)	*cālānō*	চালানো
drug	*ōshudh*	ওষুধ
drunk	*mātāl*	মাতাল
dry	*suknō*	শুকনো
dust	*dhulō/dhulā*	ধুলো / ধুলা
duty (tax)	*kor*	কর
duty	*kortobyo*	কর্তব্য

E

each	*prottek*	প্রত্যেক
early	*āge*	আগে
earn	*āyo*	আয়
earnings	*upārjon*	উপার্জ্জন
Earth	*māṭi*	মাটি
earthquake	*bhumikompo*	ভূমিকম্প
easy	*sohoj*	সহজ
eat	*khāōyā*	খাওয়া
economical	*mitobyayii*	মিতব্যয়ী
education	*shikshā*	শিক্ষা
election	*vōṭ*	ভোট
electricity	*bidyut*	বিদ্যুৎ
elevator/lift	*lifṭ*	লিফ্‌ট্
embarassment	*oprostut*	অপ্রস্তুত
embassy	*dutābās*	দূতাবাস
emergency	*jorurii*	জরুরী
empty	*khāli*	খালি
end (n)	*sesh*	শেষ

VOCABULARY

enemy	*sotru*	শত্রু
energy	*kormo sokti/tej*	কর্মশক্তি / তেজ
enormous	*birāṭ/bishāl*	বিরাট / বিশাল
enough	*jothesṭo*	যথেষ্ট
enter	*ḍhōkā/probesh*	ঢোকা / প্রবেশ
entrance	*probesh poth*	প্রবেশ পথ
equal	*somān*	সমান
etc.	*ityādi*	ইত্যাদি
evening	*sondhyā*	সন্ধ্যা
event	*ghoṭonā*	ঘটনা
every	*protyek*	প্রত্যেক
everybody	*sokole*	সকলে
everyday	*sob din/protyoho*	সবদিন / প্রত্যহ
exact	*ṭhik*	ঠিক
example	*nomunā/drisṭānto*	নমুনা / দৃষ্টান্ত
for example	*jamon*	যেমন
exception	*batikrom/chāṛā*	ব্যতিক্রম / ছাড়া
exchange (v)	*bodlānō*	বদলানো
excuse (n)	*kshomā*	ক্ষমা
exhibition	*prodorshonii*	প্রদর্শনী
exile	*nirbāson*	নির্বাসন
exit (v)	*bāhire jāyōā*	বাইরে যাওয়া
expensive	*dāmii*	দামী
experience	*oviggõtā*	অভিজ্ঞতা
expectation	*āshā*	আশা
explain (v)	*bōjhānō*	বোঝানো
export (n)	*roptānii*	রপ্তানী

F

factory	*kārkhānā*	কারখানা
fall (v)	*poṛā*	পড়া

VOCABULARY

false	*kritrim*	কৃত্রিম
family	*pōribār*	পরিবার
famous	*bikhyāto*	বিখ্যাত
fan (cooling)	*pākhā*	পাখা
far	*dur*	দুর
fast	*tāṛātāṛi/druto*	তাড়াতাড়ি / দ্রুত
fault (blame)	*dōsh*	দোষ
favourite	*priyo*	প্রিয়
fee	*mōjuri*	মজুরী
feel (v)	*lāgā/ōnuvob korā*	লাগা / অনুভব করা
female (adj)	*meyeli*	মেয়েলী
festival	*utsob*	উৎসব
fever	*jwor*	জ্বর
few	*olpo*	অল্প
fight (n)	*juddho/mārāmāri*	যুদ্ধ / মারামারি
fill (v)	*vorā*	ভরা
film (movie)	*sinemā*	সিনেমা
film (camera)	*film*	ফিল্ম
finally	*sese/obosese*	শেষে / অবশেষে
find (v)	*k̃huje pāōā*	খুঁজে পাওয়া
I can't find it.	*k̃huje pācchi nā*	খুঁজে পাচ্ছি না।
fine	*jorimānā*	জরিমানা
fire	*āgun*	আগুন
first	*prothom*	প্রথম
flag	*potākā*	পতাকা
flat (even)	*somotol*	সমতল
flea	*pōkā*	পোকা
flood	*bonnyā*	বন্যা
fog	*kuyāsā*	কুয়াসা
follow	*onusoron korā*	অনুসরন করা
food	*khābār*	খাবার

VOCABULARY

for	*jonyo*	জন্য
foreign	*bideshii*	বিদেশী
forget	*vōlā*	ভোলা
I've forgotten.	*āmi vule giyechi*	আমি ভুলে গিয়েছি
forgive	*kshomā*	ক্ষমা
former	*āger*	আগের
free (unbound)	*mukto*	মুক্ত
fresh	*tājā*	তাজা
friend	*bondhu*	বন্ধু
friendship	*bondhutwo*	বন্ধুত্ব
from	*theke*	থেকে
fruit	*fol*	ফল
full	*vōrti*	ভর্ত্তি
fun	*mojā*	মজা
funny	*mojār*	মজার
furniture	*āsbāb*	আসবাব

G

game	*khelā*	খেলা
garbage	*moyolā*	ময়লা
garden	*bāgān*	বাগান
gas	*gas*	গ্যাস
gas cylinder	*gas silindār*	গ্যাস সিলিন্ডার
generous	*doyālu*	দয়ালু
genuine	*āsol*	আসল
get up (v)	*uṭhā/ōṭhā*	উঠা / ওঠা
gift	*upohār*	উপহার
girl	*meye/bālikā*	মেয়ে / বালিকা
girlfriend	*meye bondhu*	মেয়েবন্ধু
give (v)	*deōā*	দেওয়া
Give it to me!	*āmāke dāō!*	আমাকে দাও

glasses (spectacles)	*coshmā*	চশমা
go (v)	*jāoā/colā*	যাওয়া / চলা
I'm going to ...	*āmi ... jācchi*	আমি যাচ্ছি
Where are you going?	*tumi kothāy jācchō?*	তুমি কোথায় যাচ্ছ?
God (Christian)	*goḍ*	গড্
god (Hindu)	*bhogobān/ṭhākur/ iiswor*	ভগবান / ঠাকুর / ঈশ্বর
God (Muslim)	*āllā*	আল্লা
go down (descend)	*nāmā*	নামা
gold	*sōnā*	সোনা
good	*vālō*	ভালো
Goodbye.	*bidāyo*	বিদায়
goods	*māl/jinis*	মাল / জিনিস
government	*sorkār*	সরকার
greedy	*lōvii*	লোভী
ground	*māṭi*	মাটি
group	*dol*	দল
grow	*bāṛā*	বাড়া
guess	*āndāj*	আন্দাজ
guest	*ōtithi*	অতিথি
guide (n)	*pothikrit*	পথিকৃত
guidebook	*pothoponji*	পথপঞ্জি
guilty	*dōsi*	দোষী
guitar	*giiṭār*	গিটার
gun	*bonduk*	বন্দুক

H

half	*ordhek*	অর্ধেক
handkerchief	*rumāl*	রুমাল
handsome	*sundor*	সুন্দর

happiness	*ānondo*	আনন্দ
happy	*sukhii*	সুখী
hard	*sokto/koṭhin*	শক্ত / কঠিন
hate	*ghrinā*	ঘৃণা
have (v)	*āch*	আছ
Do you have ...?	*tōmār ... āche?*	তোমার ... আছে?
I have ...	*āmār ... āche*	আমার গাড়ী আছে
health	*swāstho*	স্বাস্থ্য
hear	*sōnā*	শোনা
heater	*hiiṭār*	হীটার
heavy	*vārii*	ভারী
Hello.	*nomoskār/ādāb*	নমস্কার / আদাব।
help	*sāhājyo*	সাহায্য
Can you help me?	*āmāke ekṭu sāhājyo korben ki?*	আমাকে একটু সাহায্য করবেন কি?
here	*ekhāne*	এখানে
high	*ũchu*	উঁচু
hill	*pāhāṛ*	পাহাড়
hire	*vāṛā*	ভাড়া
I'd like to hire it.	*āmi eṭā vāṛā nebō*	আমি এটা ভাড়া নেব
history	*itihās*	ইতিহাস
hitchhike	*binā poysāi gaṛi cāpā*	বিনা পয়সায় গাড়ী চাপা
hole	*gorto*	গর্ত্ত
holiday	*chuṭi*	ছুটি
holy	*pobitro*	পবিত্র
home	*ghor/bāṛii*	ঘর / বাড়ি
homosexual	*somokāmi*	সমকামী
homesick	*baṛii mukhi*	বাড়িমুখী
honest	*sot*	সৎ

VOCABULARY

hope (n)	*āshā*	আশা
hospitality	*ātitheyotā*	আতিথেয়তা
hot	*gorom*	গরম
hotel	*hōṭel*	হোটেল
hour	*ghonṭā*	ঘন্টা
house	*bāṛii*	বাড়ি
how	*ki kōre/kamon kōre*	কি করে / কেমন করে?
How do I get to ...?	*... ki kōre jāi bōlun tō?*	কি করে যাই বলুন ত?
human	*mānobik*	মানবিক
hundred	*sho*	শ
hunger	*khide/kshudhā*	খিদে / ক্ষুধা
I'm hungry.	*āmār khide lāgche/peyeche*	আমার খিদে লাগছে. / আমার খিদেপেয়েছে
hurry, in a	*tāṛātāṛi/jōldi*	তাড়াতাড়ি / জলদি
hurt (mentally)	*obhimān*	অভিমান
hurt (physically)	*āhoto*	আহত

I

ice	*borof*	বরফ
idea	*motlob/buddhi*	মতলব. / বুদ্ধি
identification	*cinho*	চিহ্ন
idiot	*buddhu/bōkā*	বুদ্ধু. / বোকা
if	*jōdi*	যদি
ill	*osustho*	অসুস্থ
illegal	*beāinii*	বেআইনী
imagination	*kolponā*	কল্পনা
imitation	*nokol*	নকল
immediately	*akhōni/ekkhuni*	এখনি. / এক্ষুনি
import (n & v)	*āmdānii*	আমদানী
important	*dorkārii/jorurii*	দরকারী / জরুরী

impossible	*osomvob*	অসম্ভব
imprison	*bondi*	বন্দী
included	*jukto*	যুক্ত
inconvenience	*osubidhā*	অসুবিধা
incorrect	*bhul*	ভুল
increase (v)	*bāṛānō*	বাড়ানো
industry	*shilpo*	শিল্প
informal	*riti bohirvuto*	রীতি বহির্ভুত
information	*khobor*	খবর
injury	*āghāt*	আঘাত
ink	*kāli*	কালি
insect	*pōkā*	পোকা
inside/in	*vetore*	ভেতরে
insurance	*biimā*	বীমা
intelligent	*buddhimān*	বুদ্ধিমান
interest (money)	*suud*	সুদ
interest	*kōutuhol/āgroho*	কৌতুহল / আগ্রহ
I'm not interested.	*āmi āgrohii noyi*	আমি আগ্রহী নই
international	*āntorjātik*	আন্তর্যাতিক
introduce	*ālāp/poricoy*	আলাপ / পরিচয়
invitation	*āmontron/nimontron/ dāwōd* (B)	আমন্ত্রণ / নিমন্ত্রণ / দাওদ
island	*dwiip*	দ্বীপ
itch	*culkānii*	চুলকানি

J

jail	*kārāgār*	কারাগার
jaw	*cōāl*	চোয়াল
jewellery	*goyonā*	গয়না
job	*cākri*	চাকরি

VOCABULARY

joke	*ṭhāṭṭā*	ঠাট্টা
I'm joking.	*ṭhāṭṭā kōrchi*	ঠাট্টা করছি
judge (n)	*bicār poti*	বিচারপতি
judge (v)	*bicār korā*	বিচার করা
jump (v)	*lāf*	লাফ

K

key	*cābi*	চাবি
kill	*mārā*	মারা
kind (adj)	*doyālu*	দয়ালু
kind (type)	*dhoron*	ধরন
kindness	*doyā*	দয়া
kiss (n)	*cumu*	চুমু
kitchen	*rānnāghor*	রান্নাঘর
kite	*ghuṛii*	ঘুড়ি
king	*rājā*	রাজা
know (v)	*jānā*	জানা
I (don't) know.	*āmi jāni (na)*	আমি জানি না
knowledge	*gyan*	জ্ঞান

L

lake	*hrod/jhil*	হ্রদ / ঝিল
lamp	*prodip/bāti*	প্রদীপ / বাতি
land	*jomi*	জমি
landscape	*drishyo*	দৃশ্য
landslide	*dhwos*	ধ্বস
lane	*gōli*	গলি
language	*vāshā*	ভাষা
large	*boṛo*	বড়
last	*shesher*	শেষের
late	*derii*	দেরী

later on	*pore*	পরে
laugh (v)	*h̃āsā*	হাঁসা
laughter	*h̃āsi*	হাসি
law	*āyin*	আইন
lawyer	*ukiil*	উকিল
lazy	*k̃uṛe/ālse*	কুঁড়ে / আলসে
leader	*netā*	নেতা
learn	*shekhā*	শেখা
leave (v)	*chāṛā*	ছাড়া
left (direction)	*b̃ā*	বাঁ
left-wing	*bām ponthi*	বামপন্থী
legal	*āyinoto*	আইনত
lend (v)	*dhār*	ধার
lens	*k̃āc*	কাঁচ
less	*kom*	কম
letter	*ciṭhi*	চিঠি
liar	*mitthābādi*	মিথ্যাবাদী
lid	*ḍhāknā*	ঢাকনা
lie (n)	*mitthā*	মিথ্যা
lie down (v)	*shōyā*	শোয়া
life	*jiibon*	জীবন
lift/elevator	*lifṭ*	লিফ্‌ট্‌
light (ray of)	*ālō*	আলো
light (weight/ colour)	*hālkā*	হালকা
lightening	*bidyut*	বিদ্যুৎ
lighter	*opekkhākrito hālkā*	অপেক্ষাকৃত হালকা
like	*pochondo*	পছন্দ
I don't like it.	*āmār pochondo noy*	আমার পছন্দ নয়
Do you like it?	*tōmār pochondo noyecha?*	তোমার পছন্দ হয়েছে?

VOCABULARY

list (n)	*tālikā*	তালিকা
listen (v)	*shōnā*	শোনা
little	*chōṭō/olpo*	ছোট / অল্প
live (v)	*b̃ācā*	বাঁচা
lock (n)	*tālā*	তালা
long	*lombā*	লম্বা
look (v)	*dakhā*	ঢাকা
lost	*hārieche*	হারিয়েছে
I have lost ...	*āmi ... hāriechi*	আমি ... হারিয়েছি
lot	*onek/procur/bohu*	অনেক / প্রচুর / বহু
loud	*jōre*	জোরে
love (v)	*vālōbāsā*	ভালোবাসা
low	*nicu*	নীচু
luck	*vāgyo*	ভাগ্য
lucky	*vāgyobān*	ভাগ্যবান
lunch	*dupurer khābār*	দুপুরের খাবার

M

machine	*kol*	কল
mad (crazy)	*pāgol/unmād*	পাগল / উন্মাদ
mail (n)	*ḍāk*	ডাক
main	*āsol*	আসল
majority	*odhikāngso*	অধিকাংশ
make (v)	*tōiri*	তৈরী
man	*mānus*	মানুষ
many	*onek/bōhu*	অনেক / বহু
map	*māncitro*	মানচিত্র
market	*bājār*	বাজার
marriage	*biye*	বিয়ে
massage	*dolāi-mālāi*	দলাই মালাই
matches	*diāsālāyi*	দিয়াশালাই

maybe	*hoyto*	হয়ত
meal	*khābār*	খাবার
measure (n)	*māp*	মাপ
meat	*māngso*	মাংস
medical	*dāktāri*	ডাক্তারী
medicine	*ōsudh*	ওষুধ
meet (v)	*dekhā korā*	দেখা করা
memory	*smriti*	স্মৃতি
message	*khobor*	খবর
metal	*dhātu*	ধাতু
method	*upāyo*	উপায়
middle, in the	*moddhe/mājhkhāne*	মধ্যে / মাঝখানে
middle (person)	*mejō*	মেজো
mirror	*āyonā*	আয়না
mist	*kuāshā*	কুয়াশা
mistake	*bhul*	ভুল
modern	*ādhunik*	আধুনিক
moment	*muhurto*	মুহুর্ত্ত
money	*ṭākā*	টাকা
month	*mās*	মাস
monument	*smriti stombho*	স্মৃতিস্তম্ভ
moon	*cā̃d*	চাঁদ
more	*ārō*	আরো
morning	*sokāl*	সকাল
mosque	*mosjid*	মসজিদ
mountain	*porbot*	পর্ব্বত
move (v)	*noṛā*	নড়া
Mr	*sri*	শ্রী
Mrs	*shrimoti*	শ্রীমতী
much	*beshi/onek*	বেশী / অনেক
mud	*kādā*	কাদা

museum	*jādughor*	যাদুঘর
music	*gān bājnā/songiit*	গানবাজনা / সঙ্গীত

N

nail	*nokh*	নখ
name	*nām*	নাম
narcotic	*āfim*	আফিম
nation	*jāti*	জাতি
national	*jātiyo*	জাতীয়
natural	*swāvābik*	স্বাভাবিক
nature (behaviour)	*swovāb*	স্বভাব
nature	*prokriti*	প্রকৃতি
near	*kāche*	কাছে
necessary	*dorkārii*	দরকারি
need (v)	*cāōā*	চাওয়া
We need ...	*āmrā ... cāi*	আমরা ... চাই
Do you need anything? (inf)	*tomār kichu chai?*	তোমার কিছু চাই?
needle	*s̃uc*	সুঁচ
negative	*netibācok*	নেতিবাচক
never	*kokhonō nā*	কখনো না
new	*nuton*	নুতন
news	*khobor*	খবর
newspaper	*khoborer kāgoj*	খবরের কাগজ
next	*poroborti*	পরবর্তী
nice	*sundor*	সুন্দর
night	*rāt/rātri*	রাত / রাত্রি
no	*nā*	না
nobody	*keu nā*	কেউ না
noise	*sobdo/āwōāj*	শব্দ / আওয়াজ
normal	*swāvābik*	স্বাভাবিক

nothing	*kichu nā*	কিছু না
now	*akhon*	এখন
nuclear energy	*ānobik sokti*	আনবিক শক্তি
number	*sonkhyā*	সংখ্যা

O

obvious	*sposṭo*	স্পষ্ট
occupation	*jiibikā*	জীবিকা
ocean	*somudro*	সমুদ্র
offend	*coṭānō*	চটানো
offer (v)	*dān/utsorgo*	দান / উৎসর্গ
office	*doftor*	দফতর
official	*sorkāri*	সরকারী
often	*prāy*	প্রায়
oil	*tel*	তেল
old (m)	*buṛō/briddho*	বুড়ো / বৃদ্ধ
old (f)	*buṛii/briddhā*	বুড়ি / বৃদ্ধা
old (thing)	*purānō*	পুরানো
on/over	*upore*	উপরে
once	*akbār/akodā*	একবার / একদা
one	*ak/ekṭā*	এক / একটা
only	*sudhu/kebol*	শুধু / কেবল
open (v & adj)	*khulā/khōlā*	খুলা / খোলা
open minded (adj)	*udār*	উদার
opinion	*mot*	মত
opportunity	*sujōg*	সুযোগ
opposite	*ulṭā*	উল্টা
or/otherwise	*bā/othobā/kimbā*	বা / অথবা / কিম্বা
order (n)	*ādesh*	আদেশ
ordinary	*sādhāron*	সাধারন
organisation	*songsthā*	সংস্থা

organise	*babsthā*	ব্যাবস্থা
other	*onnyo*	অন্য
out/outside	*bāhire/bāire*	বাহিরে / বাইরে
oven	*unun*	উনুন
owe (v)	*dhār*	ধার
How much do I owe you?	*tōmār kāche koto dhāri?*	তোমার কাছে কত ধারি?

P

package	*puṭli*	পুট্‌লি
paddy (rice)	*dhān*	ধান
padlock	*tālā*	তালা
page	*prisṭhā*	পৃষ্ঠা
pain	*bathā/jontronā*	ব্যাথা / যন্ত্রণা
painful	*jontronā dāyok*	যন্ত্রণাদায়ক
paint (n)	*rong*	রং
pair	*jōṛā*	জোড়া
palace	*prāsād*	প্রাসাদ
paper	*kāgoj*	কাগজ
parallel	*somāntorāl*	সমান্তরাল
pardon (n)	*māf/kshomā*	মাফ / ক্ষমা
parliament	*montronā sobhā*	মন্ত্রণাসভা
participate	*ongso grohon korā*	অংশগ্রহণ করা
particular	*bisesh/nirdisṭo*	বিশেষ / নির্দিষ্ট
party (social)	*āmōd*	আমোদ
party (political)	*dol*	দল
passenger	*jātri*	যাত্রী
passport	*chāṛ potro*	ছাড়পত্র
path	*poth/rāstā*	পথ / রাস্তা
patient	*rugii*	রুগী
pay (v)	*māine deyoā*	মাইনে দেওয়া

I will pay ...	*... debo*	... দেব
peace	*shānti*	শান্তি
pen	*kolom*	কলম
people	*lōk/lōkjon*	লোক / লোকজন
perfect	*ōbikol*	অবিকল
personal	*bektigoto*	ব্যক্তিগত
personality	*bektitwo*	ব্যক্তিত্ব
perspire (v)	*ghāmā*	ঘামা
pharmacy (chemist)	*ōsudher dōkān*	ওষুধের দোকান
photograph	*foṭō*	ফটো
May I take a photo?	*ekhāne foṭō tulte pāri?*	এখানে ফটো তুলতে পারি?
piece	*ṭukrā/ongso*	টুকরা. / অংশ
place	*jāygā*	জায়গা
plan (drawing)	*noksā*	নক্সা
plain (simple)	*sādhāron*	সাধারন
plant (n)	*gāch*	গাছ
plant (v)	*rōpon*	রোপণ
play (v)	*khalā*	খেলা
Please.	*doyā kōre*	দয়া করে
plenty	*onek/jothesṭho*	অনেক / যথেষ্ট
poison	*bish*	বিষ
police station	*thānā*	থানা
politics	*rājniiti*	রাজনীতি
pollution	*dushon*	দূষণ
pond	*pukur/ḍōbā*	পুকুব / ডোবা
poor	*gorib*	গরিব
port	*bondor*	বন্দর
porter	*kuli*	কুলি
positive	*sposṭo/itibācok*	স্পষ্ট / ইতিবাচক
possible	*sombov*	সম্ভব

post (n)	*dāk*	ডাক
postage stamp	*dāk ṭikiṭ*	ডাক টিকিট
post office	*dāk ghor*	ডাকঘর
poverty	*dāridro*	দারিদ্র
practical	*byabohārik/folito*	ব্যাবহারিক / ফলিত
practice	*ōvyās*	অভ্যাস
pray	*prārthonā korā*	প্রার্থনা করা
prayer	*prārthonā*	প্রার্থনা
pregnant	*ontoswottā*	অন্তস্বত্তা
prepare (v)	*tōiri*	তৈরী
present (gift)	*upohār*	উপহার
present, to be	*uposthit*	উপস্থিত
president	*sovāpoti*	সভাপতি
pressure	*cāp*	চাপ
pretty	*sundor*	সুন্দর
prevention	*nibāron*	নিবারণ
price	*dām*	দাম
priest	*purōhit*	পুরোহিত
prime minister	*prodhān montri*	প্রধান মন্ত্রী
print (v)	*chāp*	ছাপ
prison	*kārāgār/ koyed khānā*	কারাগার / কয়েদখানা
prisoner	*koyedi*	কয়েদী
private	*baktigoto*	ব্যাক্তিগত
probably	*hoyoto/sombovoto*	হয়ত / সম্ভবত
problem	*somosyā*	সমস্যা
procession	*michil*	মিছিল
produce (n)	*fosol*	ফসল
produce (v)	*utpādon/utponno*	উপাদান / উৎপন্ন
professional	*peshādāri*	পেশাদারী
profit	*lāv*	লাভ

promise (n)	*protignā*	প্রতিজ্ঞা
pronunciation	*uccāron*	উচ্চারণ
property	*sompotti*	সম্পত্তি
prostitute	*beshyā*	বেশ্যা
protect (v)	*rokkhā korā*	রক্ষা করা
protest (n)	*protibād*	প্রতিবাদ
province	*prodesh*	প্রদেশ
psychology	*monostotwo*	মনস্তত্ত্ব
public	*sādhāroner jonyo*	সাধারনের জন্য
pull	*ṭānā*	টানা
pure	*k͠hāṭi*	খাঁটি
push	*ṭhalā/ṭhelā*	ঠ্যালা / ঠেলা
put (v)	*rākhā*	রাখা

Q

quality	*gun*	গুণ
quantity	*porimān*	পরিমান
quarrel	*jhogṛā*	ঝগড়া
quarter	*siki*	সিকি
question	*proshno/jignāsā*	প্রশ্ন / জিজ্ঞাসা
quick	*tāṛātāṛi/joldi*	তাড়াতাড়ি / জলদি
quiet	*shānto*	শান্ত

R

race (people)	*jāti*	জাতি
racism	*jātibived*	জাতিবিভেদ
radio	*betār/ākāshbāni*	বেতার / আকাশবাণী
railway	*relpoth*	রেলপথ
rain	*brisṭi*	বৃষ্টি
It's raining.	*brisṭi poṛche*	বৃষ্টি পড়ছে
rape (n)	*bolātkār*	বলাৎকার

VOCABULARY

rare	*durlov*	দুর্লভ
raw (vegetable)	*tājā*	তাজা
raw (material)	*mul*	মূল
ready	*tōiri/prostut*	তৈরী / প্রস্তুত
real	*āsol*	আসল
reason	*kāron*	কারন
recent	*ājkālkār/ādhunik*	আজকালকার / আধুনিক
receipt	*rosid*	রসিদ
receive (v)	*pāōā*	পাওয়া
refugee	*udbāstu*	উদ্বাস্তু
refund (n)	*ferot*	ফেরৎ
refuse (v)	*protyākhān*	প্রত্যাখান
region	*oncol*	অঞ্চল
relation	*sommondho*	সম্বন্ধ
relationship	*ātmiyotā*	আত্মীয়তা
religion	*dhormo*	ধর্ম
remember (v)	*mone korā*	মনে করা
rent (n)	*vāṛā*	ভাড়া
repair	*merāmot*	মেরামত
republic	*projātontro/ gonotontro*	প্রজাতন্ত্র / গণতন্ত্র
reservation	*songrokkhon*	সংরক্ষণ
reserve (v)	*songrokkhon korā*	সংরক্ষণ করা
respect (n)	*sroddhā*	শ্রদ্ধা
responsibility	*dāyitto*	দায়ীত্ব
rest	*bishrām*	বিশ্রাম
restaurant	*restorā̃/khābarer dōkān*	রেস্তোরাঁ / খাবারের / দোকান
return (v)	*ferā*	ফেরা
reverse	*ultā*	উল্টা
revolution	*biplob*	বিপ্লব

VOCABULARY

rich (wealthy)	*dhoni/boṛo lōk*	ধনী / বড়লোক
ride (v)	*coṛā*	চড়া
right (side)	*ḍān*	ডান
right (correct)	*ṭhik*	ঠিক
ring (v)	*bājānō*	বাজানো
ripe	*pākā*	পাকা
river	*nodii*	নদী
road	*rāstā*	রাস্তা
robber	*ḍākāt*	ডাকাত
rock	*pāthor/shiilā*	পাথর / শিলা
roof	*chād*	ছাদ
room	*ghor*	ঘর
rope	*doṛi*	দড়ি
round (shape)	*gōl*	গোল
rubbish	*āborjonā/jonjāl*	আবর্জনা / জঞ্জাল
ruins	*vongsostup*	ভগ্নস্তূপ
rule	*āin*	আইন
run (v)	*dōuṛānō*	দৌড়ানো

S

sad	*dukkhito/mon morā*	দুঃখিত / মন মরা
safe (adjective)	*nirāpod*	নিরাপদ
safe (n)	*sinduk*	সিন্দুক
sail (v)	*bāōā*	বাওয়া
sailor	*nābik*	নাবিক
same	*ak-i*	একই
sample	*nōmunā*	নমুনা
satisfied	*sontusṭo*	সন্তুষ্ট
say	*bolā*	বলা
Can you say that again?	*ābār bolben ki?*	আবার বলবেন কি ?

scenery	*drishyo*	দৃশ্য
sea	*sāgor/somudro*	সাগর / সমুদ্র
seasick	*somudro piiṛā*	সমুদ্রপীড়া
season	*ritu*	ঋতু
seat	*āson*	আসন
second	*dwitiyo*	দ্বিতীয়
secret	*gōpon*	গোপন
see (v)	*dakhā*	দেখা
seldom	*kodācit*	কদাচিৎ
selfish	*onudār*	অনুদার
sell	*bikrii korā*	বিক্রী করা
send	*pāṭhānō*	পাঠানো
sentence	*bākyo*	বাক্য
separate (adj & v)	*ālādā*	আলাদা
serious	*gurutto purno*	গুরুত্বপূর্ণ
serve (v)	*pōribeshon*	পরিবেশন
sew	*selāi korā*	সেলাই করা
shade	*chāyā*	ছায়া
shape	*ākār*	আকার
share (v)	*bhāg korā*	ভাগ করা
shave	*kāmānō*	কামানো
shell (sea)	*jhinuk*	ঝিনুক
ship	*jāhāj*	জাহাজ
shop	*dōkān*	দোকান
shore	*tiir*	তীর
short (height)	*b̃eṭe/chōṭō*	বেঁটে / ছোট
shortage	*durlov*	দুর্লভ
show (v)	*dakhā*	দেখা
Show me!	*āmāke dakhāo!*	আমাকে দেখাও
shut (v)	*bondho korā*	বন্ধ করা
shy	*lājuk*	লাজুক

sick	*osustho*	অসুস্থ
sign (symbol)	*cinho*	চিহ্ন
signature	*soi*	সই
similar	*somān*	সমান
simple	*sohoj*	সহজ
since	*theke*	থেকে
sing	*gāōā*	গাওয়া
sit	*bosā*	বসা
situation	*obosthā*	অবস্থা
size	*māp*	মাপ
skin	*cāmṛā*	চামড়া
sky	*ākās*	আকাশ
sleep (v)	*ghumānō*	ঘুমানো
slow	*dhiir*	ধীর
slowly	*āste*	আস্তে
small	*chōṭō*	ছোট
smell (n)	*gondho*	গন্ধ
smile (n)	*h̃āsi*	হাঁসি
snow	*borof*	বরফ
soap	*sābān*	সাবান
socialism	*somāj tontro*	সমাজতন্ত্র
soft	*norom*	নরম
soil	*māṭi*	মাটি
soldier	*sōinik*	সৈনিক
solid	*kōṭhin*	কঠিন
somebody	*keu*	কেউ
some/something	*kichu*	কিছু
somewhere	*kōthāō*	কোথাও
song	*gān*	গান
soon	*sighro/siggiir*	শীঘ্র /শীগগীর
sorry	*dukkhito*	দুখিতঃ

I'm sorry.	*āmi dukkhito*	আমি দুখিতঃ
space	*jāyogā*	জায়গা
speak	*bolā*	বলা
I can't speak Bengali.	*āmi Bānglā bolte pāri nā*	আমি বাংলা বলতে পারি না
special	*bishesh*	বিশেষ
sport	*khelā*	খেলা
stairs	*s̃iṛi*	সিঁড়ি
stale	*biswād*	বিস্বাদ
stamp (v)	*chāp*	ছাপ
stamp (postage)	*dāk ṭikiṭ*	ডাকটিকিট
stand (v)	*d̃āṛānō*	দাঁড়ানো
standard	*mān*	মান
star	*tārā*	তারা
start (n)	*suru*	শুরু
stay	*thākā*	থাকা
steal	*curi korā*	চুরি করা
steam	*bāshpo*	বাষ্প
steep	*khāṛā*	খাড়া
stick	*lāṭhi/choṛi*	লাঠি / ছড়ি
still (yet)	*akhono/tothāpi/tōbu*	এখনো / তথাপি / তবু
stone	*pāthor*	পাথর
stop (v)	*thāmānō/bondho korā*	থামানো / বন্ধ করা
storm	*jhoṛ*	ঝড়
storey	*tolā*	তলা
story	*golpo*	গল্প
straight	*sōjā*	সোজা
strange	*odvut*	অদ্ভুত
stranger	*āgontuk*	আগন্তুক
street	*rāstā*	রাস্তা

VOCABULARY

string	*sutā/dōṛi*	সুতা / দড়ি
strong (person)	*sōktishāli*	শক্তিশালী
strong (adj)	*sokto*	শক্ত
student	*chātro*	ছাত্র
study (v)	*poṛā*	পড়া
stupid	*buddhu/bōkā*	বুদ্ধু / বোকা
substance	*jinish*	জিনিষ
successful	*sofol*	সফল
suddenly	*hoṭhāt*	হঠাৎ
sun	*surjo*	সূর্য
sure	*niscoy*	নিশ্চয়
I will (surely) come.	*āmi (niscoy) āsbō*	আমি (নিশ্চয়) আসব
surprise (n)	*bismoy*	বিস্ময়
survive	*b̃ācā*	বাঁচা
sweet	*misṭi*	মিষ্টি
swim (v)	*s̃ātār*	সাঁতার

T

tailor	*dorji*	দরজি
take	*neōā*	নেওয়া
talk (v)	*bolā*	বলা
tall	*lombā*	লম্বা
tap (water)	*kʋl*	কল
tape	*fitā*	ফিতা
taste (v)	*c̃ākhā*	চাঁখা
taste (n)	*swād*	স্বাদ
tax	*kor*	কর
teach	*poṛānō*	পড়ানো
team	*dol*	দল
tell	*bolā*	বলা

VOCABULARY

temperature	*tāp*	তাপ
temple	*mondir*	মন্দির
than	*theke/ceye/opekkhā*	থেকে / চেয়ে / অপেক্ষা
Thank you.	*dhonyobād*	ধন্যবাদ
there	*sekhāne/ōkhāne*	সেখানে / ওখানে
thick	*ghono* (liquid)/ *puru/mōṭā*	ঘন / পুরু / মোটা
thief	*cōr*	চোর
thin	*pātlā/soru*	পাতলা / সরু
thing	*jinish*	জিনিস
think (v)	*cintā korā*	চিন্তা করা
third	*tritiiyo*	তৃতীয়
thirst	*tesṭā/pipāsā*	তেষ্টা / পিপাসা
thread	*sutā*	সুতা
through	*diye/hōye*	দিয়ে / হয়ে
throw	*c̃hōṛā*	ছোঁড়া
thunder	*bojjro*	বজ্র
tide (high)	*jōār*	জোয়ার
tide (low)	*ṽāṭā*	ভাঁটা
tie (v)	*b̃ādhā*	বাঁধা
tight	*sokto*	শক্ত
tight (clothes)	*ã̄ṭ*	আঁট
time	*somoy*	সময়
What time is it?	*koṭā bāje/akhon somoi koto?*	কটা বাজে / এখন সময় কত ?
tip (gratuity)	*bokhsish*	বখশিশ
tired	*klānto*	ক্লান্ত
I'm tired.	*āmi klānto*	আমি ক্লান্ত
to	*proti/porjyonto/dike*	প্রতি / পর্যন্ত / দিকে
today	*āj*	আজ
together	*songe*	সঙ্গে

toilet	*pāykhānā*	পায়খানা
tomorrow	*(āgāmii) kāl*	(আগামী) কাল
top	*upore*	উপরে
touch (v)	*chõyā*	ছোঁয়া
tour	*vromon/sofar/ pōrjōṭon*	ভ্রমণ / সফর. / পর্য্যটন
tourist	*vromonkāri*	ভ্রমণকারী
towards	*dike*	দিকে
town	*sohor*	সহর
toy	*khelnā*	খেলনা
translation	*onubād*	অনুবাদ
travel	*vromon*	ভ্রমণ
trouble	*bipod/muskil*	বিপদ / মুশকিল
true	*sotyi*	সত্যি
trust	*biswās*	বিশ্বাস
try	*cesṭā*	চেষ্টা
turn (v)	*ghōrā/firā*	ঘোরা / ফিরা
twice	*du bār*	দুবার

U

ugly	*kutsit/bishrii*	কুৎসিত / বিশ্রী
umbrella	*chātā*	ছাতা
uncomfortable	*osojhyo*	অসহ্য
under	*niice/tolāyo*	নীচে / তলায়
understand	*bujhā*	বুঝা
I (don't) understand.	*bujhte pārlām (nā)*	বুঝতে পারলাম (না)
unemployed	*bekār*	বেকার
university	*biswobidyāloy*	বিশ্ববিদ্যালয়
unsafe (dangerous)	*bipojjonok*	বিপজ্জনক
until	*porjonto*	পর্যন্ত

VOCABULARY

up/upstairs	*upore*	উপরে
urgent	*jorurii*	জরুরী
use (v)	*babohār korā*	ব্যবহার করা
useful	*dorkāri/proyōjoniyo*	দরকারী / প্রয়োজনীয়
usually	*pray-i*	প্রায়ই

V

vacant	*khāli*	খালি
vacation	*chuṭi*	ছুটি
vaccination	*ṭikā*	টিকা
valley	*utrāi*	উৎরাই
value	*dām*	দাম
valuable	*dāmii*	দামী
vegetable	*sobjii*	সবজী
very	*khub/otyonto/ viishon*	খুব / অত্যন্ত / ভীষণ
via	*hōye*	হয়ে
view (n)	*drisyo*	দৃশ্য
village	*grām*	গ্রাম
visit (n)	*poridorshon/ āgomon*	পরিদর্শন / আগমন
visit (v)	*poridorshon korā*	পরিদর্শন করা
visitor	*porjyoṭok*	পর্যটক
vomit	*bōmi*	বমি
vote	*vōt*	ভোট

W

wait	*opekshā*	অপেক্ষা
Please wait.	*ekṭu opekkhā korun*	একটু অপেক্ষা করুন
wage	*māine*	মাইনে
wake (v)	*jāgā*	জাগা
walk (v)	*hā̃ṭā/colā*	হাঁটা / চলা

wall	*dewāl*	দেয়াল
want (v)	*cāyōā*	চাওয়া
I/We want ...	*āmi/āmrā cāi*	আমি / আমরা চাই
Do you want ...?	*āpni cān ki?*	আপনি চান কি?
war	*juddho*	যুদ্ধ
warm	*gorom/ushno*	গরম / উষ্ম
wash (v)	*dhōyā*	ধোয়া
watch (v)	*dakhā*	দেখা
watch (n)	*ghōṛi*	ঘড়ি
water	*jol/pāni* (B)	জল / পানি
waterfall	*jolopropāt*	জলপ্রপাত
way (method)	*upāyo*	উপায়
way (road)	*rāstā*	রাস্তা
Which way?	*kōn rāstāi*	কোন রাস্তায়?
weak	*durbol*	দুর্ব্বল
wealthy	*dhonii/boṛolōk*	ধনী / বড়লোক
wear	*porā*	পরা
weather	*ābhāyōā*	আবহাওয়া
wedding	*biye*	বিয়ে
week	*soptāho/hoptā*	সপ্তাহ / হপ্তা
weigh	*ōjon korā*	ওজন করা
Welcome!	*swāgotom!*	স্বাগতম
well (waterhole)	*k̃uā*	কুঁয়া
well (adj)	*vālo*	ভালো
wet	*vejā*	ভেজা
what	*ki*	কি
What is that?	*eke ki bole?*	একে কি বলে?
whatever	*jākichu*	যা কিছু
wheel	*cākā*	চাকা
when	*kokhon*	কখন

When does the bus leave?	*kokhon bās chāre?*	কখন বাস ছাড়ে?
where	*kōthāyo*	কোথায়
Where is ...?	*... kōthāy?*	... কোথায়?
which	*kōn*	কোন
Which one?	*kōnṭā?*	কোনটা?
while	*jokhon*	যখন
who	*ke*	কে
Who is it?	*uni ke?*	উনি কে?
whoever	*je keu*	যে কেউ
whole	*somosto*	সমস্ত
why	*kano*	কেন
wide	*coyōṛā/prosostho*	চওড়া / প্রশস্ত
wild	*bonnyo*	বন্য
win	*jetā*	জেতা
wind (n)	*bātās/hāyōā*	বাতাস / হাওয়া
wise	*gyani*	জ্ঞানী
with	*songe*	সঙ্গে
without	*chāṛā/bāde*	ছাড়া / বাদে
woman	*nārii/strilōk/meye mānush*	নারী / স্ত্রীলোক / মেয়ে মানুষ
wood	*kāṭh*	কাঠ
word	*shobdo*	শব্দ
word (news)	*khobor*	খবর
work (n)	*kāj*	কাজ
world	*prithibii*	পৃথিবী
wound	*kshoto*	ক্ষত
wrap	*joṛānō*	জড়ানো
write	*lekhā*	লেখা
wrong	*bhul*	ভুল

VOCABULARY

Y

year	*bochor*	বছর
yes	*ĥa/ĥā/ĥu*	হ্যাঁ / হাঁ / হুঁ
yet	*tōbu/tothāpi*	তবু / তথাপি
yesterday	*(goto)kāl*	(গত) কাল
young	*chōṭō/koci*	ছোট / কচি

Z

zeal	*utsāho*	উৎসাহ
zero	*shunyo*	শুণ্য
zone	*elākā*	এলাকা
zoo	*ciṛiākhānā*	চিড়িয়াখানা

Emergencies

Help!	*b̃ācāō!*	বাঁচাও!
Police!	*pulish!*	পুলিশ!
Thief!	*cōr!*	চোর!
Go away!	*bhāgō!*	ভাগো!
Fire!	*āgun!*	আগুন!
Careful/Beware!	*sābdhān!*	সাবধান!
Pickpocket!	*pokeṭmār!*	পকেটমার!

I've been in an accident!
āmi ak durghoṭonāyo poṛechi! — আমি এক দুর্ঘটনায় পড়েছি

Call a doctor!
ḍaktār ḍakun! — ডাক্তার ডাকুন!

Call an ambulance!
ambulans ḍakun! — এ্যাম্বুলেন্স্ ডাকুন!

Call the police!
pulis ḍakun! — পুলিশ ডাকুন!

I've been robbed of everything.
āmār sobkichu curi giyeche. — আমার সবকিছু চুরি গিয়েছে

I've lost my ...	*āmār ... curi giyeche*	আমার ... চুরি গিয়েছে
jewellery	*gohonā*	গয়না
money	*ṭākā*	টাকা
passport	*paspōrṭ*	পাসপোর্ট

wallet	*ōāleṭ*	ওয়ালেট
watch	*ghōṛi*	ঘড়ি

I am lost.
āmi poth hāriyechi — আমি পথ হারিয়েছি

I'm terribly sorry.
āmi khub dukkhito — আমি খুব দুখিঃত

I didn't realise I was doing anything wrong.
āmi bujhini je āmi onnyāo kichu korchi — আমি বুঝিনি যে আমি অন্যায় কিছু করেছি

I didn't do it.
āmi korini — আমি করিনি

I want to contact my embassy/consulate.
āmi dutābāser songe jōgājōg korte cāi — আমি দুতাবাসের সঙ্গে যোগাযোগ করতে চাই

Index

LONELY PLANET

Phrasebooks

Lonely Planet phrasebooks are packed with essential words and phrases to help travellers communicate with the locals. With colour tabs for quick reference, an extensive vocabulary and use of script, these handy pocket-sized language guides cover day-to-day travel situations.

- handy pocket-sized books
- easy to understand Pronunciation chapter
- clear & comprehensive Grammar chapter
- romanisation alongside script to allow ease of pronunciation
- script throughout so users can point to phrases for every situation
- full of cultural information and tips for the traveller

'... vital for a real DIY spirit and attitude in language learning'

– *Backpacker*

'the phrasebooks have good cultural backgrounders and offer solid advice for challenging situations in remote locations'

– *San Francisco Examiner*

Australian *(Australian English, Aboriginal & Torres Strait languages)* • Baltic *(Estonian, Latvian, Lithuanian)* • Bengali • Brazilian • British *(English, dialects, Scottish Gaelic, Welsh)* • Burmese • Cantonese • Central Asia *(Kazakh, Kyrgyz, Pashto, Tajik, Tashkorghani, Turkmen, Uyghur, Uzbek & others)* • Central Europe *(Czech, German, Hungarian, Polish, Slovak, Slovene)* • Costa Rica Spanish • Czech • Eastern Europe *(Albanian, Bulgarian, Croatian, Czech, Hungarian, Macedonian, Polish, Romanian, Serbian, Slovak, Slovene)* • East Timor *(Tetun, Portuguese)* • Egyptian Arabic • Ethiopian (Amharic) • Europe *(Basque, Catalan, Dutch, French, German, Greek, Irish, Italian, Maltese, Portuguese, Scottish Gaelic, Spanish, Turkish, Welsh)* • Farsi (Persian) • Fijian • French • German • Greek • Hebrew • Hill Tribes *(Lahu, Akha, Lisu, Mong, Mien & others)* • Hindi & Urdu • Indonesian • Italian • Japanese • Korean • Lao • Latin American Spanish • Malay • Mandarin • Mongolian • Moroccan Arabic • Nepali • Pidgin • Pilipino (Tagalog) • Polish • Portuguese • Quechua • Russian • Scandinavian *(Danish, Faroese, Finnish, Icelandic, Norwegian, Swedish)* • South-East Asia *(Burmese, Indonesian, Khmer, Lao, Malay, Pilipino (Tagalog), Thai, Vietnamese)* • South Pacific *(Fijian, Hawaiian, Kanak languages, Maori, Niuean, Rapanui, Rarotongan Maori, Samoan, Tahitian, Tongan & others)* • Spanish *(Castilian, also includes Catalan, Galician & Basque)* • Sinhala • Swahili • Thai • Tibetan • Turkish • Ukrainian • USA *(US English, vernacular, Native American, Hawaiian)* • Vietnamese

COMPLETE LIST OF LONELY PLANET BOOKS

AFRICA Africa on a shoestring • Cairo • Cape Town • East Africa • Egypt • Ethiopia, Eritrea & Djibouti • The Gambia & Senegal • Healthy Travel Africa • Kenya • Malawi • Morocco • Mozambique • Read This First: Africa • South Africa, Lesotho & Swaziland • Southern Africa • Southern Africa Road Atlas • Tanzania, Zanzibar & Pemba • Trekking in East Africa • Tunisia • Watching Wildlife East Africa • Watching Wildlife Southern Africa • West Africa • World Food Morocco • Zimbabwe, Botswana & Namibia

AUSTRALIA & THE PACIFIC Aboriginal Australia & the Torres Strait Islands • Auckland • Australia • Australia Road Atlas • Bushwalking in Australia • Cycling Australia • Cycling New Zealand • Fiji • Healthy Travel Australia, NZ and the Pacific • Islands of Australia's Great Barrier Reef • Melbourne • Micronesia • New Caledonia • New South Wales & the ACT • New Zealand • Northern Territory • Outback Australia • Out to Eat – Melbourne • Out to Eat – Sydney • Papua New Guinea • Queensland • Rarotonga & the Cook Islands • Samoa • Solomon Islands • South Australia • South Pacific • Sydney • Sydney Condensed • Tahiti & French Polynesia • Tasmania • Tonga • Tramping in New Zealand • Vanuatu • Victoria • Walking in Australia • Watching Wildlife Australia • Western Australia

CENTRAL AMERICA & THE CARIBBEAN Bahamas, Turks & Caicos • Baja California • Bermuda • Central America on a shoestring • Costa Rica • Cuba • Dominican Republic & Haiti • Eastern Caribbean • Guatemala • Guatemala, Belize & Yucatán: La Ruta Maya • Havana • Healthy Travel Central & South America • Jamaica • Mexico • Mexico City • Panama • Puerto Rico • Read This First: Central & South America • World Food Mexico • Yucatán

EUROPE Amsterdam • Amsterdam Condensed • Andalucía • Austria • Barcelona • Belgium & Luxembourg • Berlin • Britain • Brussels, Bruges & Antwerp • Budapest • Canary Islands • Central Europe •Copenhagen • Corfu & the Ionians • Corsica • Crete • Crete Condensed • Croatia • Cycling Britain • Cycling France • Cyprus • Czech & Slovak Republics • Denmark • Dublin • Eastern Europe • Edinburgh • England • Estonia, Latvia & Lithuania • Europe on a shoestring • Finland • Florence • France • Frankfurt Condensed • Georgia, Armenia & Azerbaijan • Germany • Greece • Greek Islands • Hungary • Iceland, Greenland & the Faroe Islands • Ireland • Istanbul • Italy • Krakow • Lisbon • The Loire • London • London Condensed • Madrid • Malta • Mediterranean Europe • Milan, Turin & Genoa • Moscow • Mozambique • Munich • The Netherlands • Normandy • Norway • Out to Eat – London • Paris • Paris Condensed • Poland • Portugal • Prague • Provence & the Côte d'Azur • Read This First: Europe • Rhodes & the Dodecanese • Romania & Moldova • Rome • Rome Condensed • Russia, Ukraine & Belarus • Scandinavian & Baltic Europe • Scotland • Sicily • Slovenia • South-West France • Spain • St Petersburg • Sweden • Switzerland • Trekking in Spain • Tuscany • Venice • Vienna • Walking in Britain • Walking in France • Walking in Ireland • Walking in Italy • Walking in Spain • Walking in Switzerland • Western Europe • World Food France • World Food Ireland • World Food Italy • World Food Spain

COMPLETE LIST OF LONELY PLANET BOOKS

INDIAN SUBCONTINENT Bangladesh • Bhutan • Delhi • Goa • Healthy Travel Asia & India • India • Indian Himalaya • Karakoram Highway • Kerala • Mumbai (Bombay) • Nepal • Pakistan • Rajasthan • Read This First: Asia & India • South India • Sri Lanka • Tibet • Trekking in the Indian Himalaya • Trekking in the Karakoram & Hindukush • Trekking in the Nepal Himalaya

ISLANDS OF THE INDIAN OCEAN Madagascar &Comoros • Maldives • Mauritius, Réunion & Seychelles

MIDDLE EAST & CENTRAL ASIA Bahrain, Kuwait & Qatar • Central Asia • Dubai • Iran • Israel & the Palestinian Territories • Istanbul • Istanbul to Cairo on a Shoestring • Istanbul to Kathmandu • Jerusalem • Jordan • Lebanon • Middle East • Oman & the United Arab Emirates • Syria • Turkey • World Food Turkey • Yemen

NORTH AMERICA Alaska • Boston • Boston Condensed • British Colombia • California & Nevada • California Condensed • Canada • Chicago • Deep South • Florida • Great Lakes • Hawaii • Hiking in Alaska • Hiking in the USA • Honolulu • Las Vegas • Los Angeles • Louisiana & The Deep South • Miami • Montreal • New England • New Orleans • New York City • New York City Condensed • New York, New Jersey & Pennsylvania • Oahu • Out to Eat – San Francisco • Pacific Northwest • Puerto Rico • Rocky Mountains • San Francisco • San Francisco Map • Seattle • Southwest • Texas • Toronto • USA • Vancouver • Virginia & the Capital Region • Washington DC • World Food Deep South, USA • World Food New Orleans

NORTH-EAST ASIA Beijing • China • Hiking in Japan • Hong Kong • Hong Kong Condensed • Hong Kong, Macau & Guangzhou • Japan • Korea • Kyoto • Mongolia • Seoul • Shanghai • South-West China • Taiwan • Tokyo • World Food – Hong Kong

SOUTH AMERICA Argentina, Uruguay & Paraguay • Bolivia • Brazil • Buenos Aires • Chile & Easter Island • Colombia • Ecuador & the Galapagos Islands • Healthy Travel Central & South America • Peru • Read This First: Central & South America • Rio de Janeiro • Santiago • South America on a shoestring • Santiago • Trekking in the Patagonian Andes • Venezuela

SOUTH-EAST ASIA Bali & Lombok • Bangkok • Cambodia • Hanoi • Healthy Travel Asia & India • Ho Chi Minh City • Indonesia • Indonesia's Eastern Islands • Jakarta • Java • Laos • Malaysia, Singapore & Brunei • Myanmar (Burma) • Philippines • Read This First: Asia & India • Singapore • South-East Asia on a shoestring • Thailand • Thailand's Islands & Beaches • Thailand, Vietnam, Laos & Cambodia Road Atlas • Vietnam • World Food Thailand • World Food Vietnam

Also available; Journeys travel literature, illustrated pictorials, calendars, diaries, Lonely Planet maps and videos. For more information on these series and for the complete range of Lonely Planet products and services, visit our website at **www.lonelyplanet.com**.

LONELY PLANET

Series Description

travel guidebooks	in depth coverage with background and recommendations download selected guidebook Upgrades at www.lonelyplanet.com
shoestring guides	for travellers with more time than money
condensed guides	highlights the best a destination has to offer
citySync	digital city guides for Palm TM OS
outdoor guides	walking, cycling, diving and watching wildlife
phrasebooks	don't just stand there, say something!
city maps and road atlases	essential navigation tools
world food	for people who live to eat, drink and travel
out to eat	a city's best places to eat and drink
read this first	invaluable pre-departure guides
healthy travel	practical advice for staying well on the road
journeys	travel stories for armchair explorers
pictorials	lavishly illustrated pictorial books
ekno	low cost international phonecard with e-services
TV series and videos	on the road docos
web site	for chat, Upgrades and destination facts
lonely planet images	on line photo library

LONELY PLANET OFFICES

Australia
Locked Bag 1, Footscray,
Victoria 3011
☎ 03 8379 8000
fax 03 8379 8111
email: talk2us@lonelyplanet.com.au

UK
72 82 Roseberry Ave,
London EC1R 4RW
☎ 020 7841 9000
fax 020 7841 9001
email: go@lonelyplanet.co.uk

USA
150 Linden St, Oakland,
CA 94607
☎ 510 893 8555
TOLL FREE: 800 275 8555
fax 510 893 8572
email: info@lonelyplanet.com

France
1 rue du Dahomey,
75011 Paris
☎ 01 55 25 33 00
fax 01 55 25 33 01
email: bip@lonelyplanet.fr
website: www.lonelyplanet.fr

World Wide Web: www.lonelyplanet.com *or* AOL keyword: lp
Lonely Planet Images: lpi@lonelyplanet.com.au